THE SKY'S THE LIMIT

THE SKY'S THE LIMIT

THE STORY OF VICKY JACK AND HER QUEST TO CLIMB THE SEVEN SUMMITS

ANNA MAGNUSSON

BLACK & WHITE PUBLISHING

First published 2007
by Black & White Publishing Ltd
99 Giles Street, Edinburgh EH6 6BZ

1 3 5 7 9 10 8 6 4 2 07 08 09 10 11

ISBN 13: 978 1 84502 171 9
ISBN 10: 1 84502 171 1

Quote from Joe Simpson in Prologue:
From his introduction to *Annapurna* by Maurice Herzog (Pimlico 1997).
Introduction to Pimlico edition, copyright Joe Simpson 1997

Quote from Ithaka by C. P. Cavafy in Epilogue:
From *Collected Poems* (Chatto & Windus, 1990), translated by Edmund
Keeley and Philip Sherrard

A CIP catalogue record for this book
is available from the British Library.

Typeset by Ellipsis Books Limited, Glasgow

Printed and bound by MPG Books Ltd, Bodmin, Cornwall

ACKNOWLEDGEMENTS

'She looks as if a puff of wind will blow her away' is how one old friend describes Vicky Jack.

Appearances can be deceptive, as I have found out during the months of talking to Vicky and writing her story for this book. She wears her achievement in climbing the Seven Summits so lightly as to render it almost invisible but, as I've come to know her, I've been enormously impressed and inspired by her talents, her personality and her great appetite for life. She has been unstinting in her time and efforts over these past months as we've talked about her life and career and climbing – always thoughtful and always open and I thank her most sincerely. Although we first met nearly two years ago, our conversations and my writing of the book have taken place during a very intensive period of only three or four months. It has been exhausting but Vicky has never once flagged along the way. That's probably why she got to the top of Everest . . .

I would also like to thank the many people – friends, family, climbing chums, work colleagues – who have helped me with information, stories, reflections and memories. I hope that the Vicky you find in this book is, at least in small part, the Vicky you know.

Thank you, Mum, for all the hours you spent going over each chapter and making suggestions and corrections.

Thank you, Julie, for all your love and support over these long months. This book is also for you.

Anna Magnusson

For Dad

Who said to me one day two years ago,
'Dearest, I've just met a very interesting woman called
Vicky Jack. You should write a book about her.'

Here it is, Dad.

Magnus Magnusson, 1929–2007

CONTENTS

FOREWORD   xi

PROLOGUE   1

1   IN THE GARDEN   6

2   TRAVELLING   21

3   THE HIGHEST HILL IN EUROPE
     MOUNT ELBRUS   37

4   UNDER AFRICAN SKIES
     KILIMANJARO   52

5   HIGH IN THE ANDES
     ACONCAGUA   61

6   THE WHITE SOUTH
     VINSON MASSIF   77

7   THE HARDEST JOURNEY
     MOUNT McKINLEY   101

8   THE DARK MOUNTAIN
     CARSTENSZ PYRAMID   119

9   THE ROAD TO EVEREST   144

10   THE HIGHEST MOUNTAIN IN THE WORLD
     MOUNT EVEREST   162

11   ON TOP OF THE WORLD   195

EPILOGUE   208

FOREWORD

After I had completed the Seven Summits, I was asked if I was going to write a book about 'my adventures'. I knew that what I really enjoyed was the adventuring and not writing so I decided to look for someone to write the book for me. Never having delved into the book-writing world before, it took some time and, just when I was starting to make progress, I was awarded an honorary doctorate from Glasgow Caledonian University. Magnus Magnusson was the university's chancellor at the time and, during the pre-award-ceremony lunch, I was sitting next to him. We were chatting and he suddenly put his hand on my arm and, with an excited boyish look, said that his daughter Anna wanted to write another book and he thought that my story would be ideal for her. He asked if it would be all right for him to suggest it to her and of course I said, 'Yes.'

I then met Anna and she was not only keen to write about the adventures but also wanted to cover my life. I found this prospect quite daunting as I am not one to discuss my experiences, feelings and emotions, particularly with someone I didn't know. However, when we met, I immediately liked Anna – she has a quiet confidence, a good sense of humour and is very insightful. I felt that I could trust her to write a true account of my story and we agreed to go ahead.

It was a lot harder than I thought it would be but the hours spent talking about my past were made so much easier by Anna's relaxed patience and perceptive questioning.

I tend to make light of things but, underneath, there is a serious person and Anna was swift to discover this. In fact, I

think now she probably knows me better than I know myself!
Thanks, Anna – you have captured my life astonishingly well.

I would also like to thank Anna's mother Mamie and her
sister Margaret for giving honest and constructive feedback as
each chapter was written.

And of course thanks to everyone we contacted who so
enthusiastically added their accounts to the book.

I believe we tend to limit our own horizons but I also believe
that, if you really want to do something and you feel it from
your heart, you can achieve almost anything – the sky's the
limit!

I hope you enjoy the book.

Vicky Jack

PROLOGUE

They are ... for me, sources of wonder, of life-enhancing
moments when the borders between living and dying seem to
overlap, when the past and the future cease to exist and you
are free.

Joe Simpson describing his relationship with mountains

From his Introduction to *Annapurna*

by Maurice Herzog (1997)

As light began to smudge the horizon on 22 May 2003, Vicky
Jack stood at 27,500 feet on Mount Everest, about 1,500 vertical
feet from the summit.

It was a beautiful dawn. The weather was superb, there were
no clouds, and I cried with the sheer impact of seeing the
dawn growing, looking down on everything. We were above
every hill around us. You could see the curvature of the Earth.
I could hear the oxygen coming through the pipe beside my
ear. I could hear my own ragged gasps for breath. I was
absolutely exhausted, but there was this sudden feeling of
elation: and that split second of feeling will never leave me.

That day on Everest was the planned culmination of her
six-year quest to climb the Seven Summits, the highest peaks
on the seven continents: Mount Elbrus in the Caucasus;
Kilimanjaro in Tanzania; Aconcagua in the Andes; the Vinson
Massif in Antarctica; Mount McKinley (also known as Denali)
in Alaska; Carstensz Pyramid (also known as Puncak Jaya) in

Indonesia; and Mount Everest in Nepal. There is some debate about which are the seven highest peaks, and there are two rival lists. Some people climb Mount Kosciuszko in Australia instead of Carstensz (see pages 52–53). When Vicky climbed Mount Everest in 2003 she was fifty, a fit, wiry, slight woman who had a successful career in human resources and had recently set up her own HR consultancy. She'd already had many adventures climbing the highest mountains all over the world, from Alaska to Antarctica: she'd spent a night being very sick in the freezing cold on Mount Elbrus and had nearly died in a blizzard in Antarctica after summiting the Vinson Massif; she'd fallen off a narrow ledge 16,000 feet up on Mount McKinley in Alaska; and, in 2001, she'd been smuggled in a speeding truck through the world's largest open-cast mine (where no women, let alone tourists, were allowed), en route to climbing the Carstensz Pyramid in Papua, Indonesia. And here on Everest was the ultimate challenge, the final test of her determination to push herself to the limits of her mental and physical strength.

Forty-three years earlier Vicky had been on a different hill, a tiny mound by comparison, on a childhood holiday in the Scottish Highlands. She and her brother, Brian, were climbing Ben Bhuidhe with their parents. They raced up the hill in great excitement and Vicky's father called to them to sit down and not get too far ahead. So the children were laughing and giggling, bumping their way up the hill backwards on their bottoms, shouting to Mum and Dad below to hurry up. They were so slow! Later that day, skipping down off the hill, Vicky was thrilled and scared when she and Brian found a dead wildcat which had been hung from a barbed wire fence, by the farmer presumably, to warn off other predators.

Ben Bhuidhe was Vicky's first Munro (a hill over 3,000 feet), her first proper hill. The personal and inspirational journey from that first climb, all the way to the summits of the highest mountains in the world, including Everest, is the story of this book. Vicky is not an elite mountaineer, and this book is not about mountaineering. It is about how hills and mountains have been an inspirational part of her life. Vicky is one of us, and her life has been like millions of ordinary lives – a middle-class background, an unexceptional childhood, a career – except for the fact that a comfortable life and successful career weren't enough. Always there was the pull and the drive to test her limits, to live her life to the full. 'I believe in going for life and giving it your all,' she says. 'I've always believed in that.' And so she began a ten-year plan to climb all Scotland's Munros, which was wonderful when she was doing it because it gave her something to aim for and a sense of purpose outside her enormously demanding work; but, when she completed the final one, she felt rudderless and needed another challenge. One night, in a pub with some friends, she was talking about this and somebody said, 'Why don't you climb the highest hill in Europe?' Months later, on the descent from Mount Elbrus, one of the team asked, 'Are you doing the Seven Summits, then?' 'I don't know,' replied Vicky. 'What are they?' From that moment she was hooked. The next seven years of her life would be devoted to achieving her goal.

But on that day in May 2003, within reach of the summit of Everest, within an hour and a half of realising her dream, Vicky turned back. The weather had changed and was threatening, she was exhausted, there was a queue of people waiting to get up the Hillary Step and somewhere in the midst of her oxygen-deprived consciousness, an instinct told her to turn back. Weeks and weeks of climbing and acclimatisation, a great deal of money to pay for the trip, years of mental and physical preparation for this yearned-for moment – and she turned back.

So near and yet so far. Three hundred vertical feet away from the summit, and I had to turn back. The weather was bad and getting worse and the wind was blowing me over. I wasn't capable of making a rational decision at that altitude. It was an instinct. So I turned back. I still think it was the right decision to have made. I've never regretted turning back.

She promised she would return the following year, somehow, and try again. And she did. In May 2004, at the age of fifty-one, she became the oldest British woman to summit Everest and the first Scottish woman to complete the Seven Summits.

Vicky doesn't call herself a climber – she's a 'high hill walker'; she won't call the peaks she's summited mountains – 'that's too scary' – so she calls them hills. She describes herself as an ordinary woman who pushes herself to achieve the extraordinary things many of the rest of us dream about as we sit in offices or stuck in traffic, making ends meet, holding on to security – if only we had the time, the energy, the drive, the money. Vicky herself says that if she'd settled down years ago and had a family as well as a career, she might not have been driven to search for the fulfilment and peace and sense of achievement which lie at the heart of her mountain climbing.

As a woman, she has pursued her dream very much in a man's world – on most expeditions to the Seven Summits she was the only woman. She's had to match men physically in the most gruelling and hostile natural environments, and has held her own in an intensely competitive, male-dominated sport. Wrapped up under impenetrable layers of fleece and a down suit in the Antarctic, she cheerfully admits that she's been just one of the boys. And when she embarked on the Seven Summits she was also looking after her widowed mother, driving the 100 miles each weekend from her home in Aviemore to Balquhidder where her mother lived on her own.

The high mountains of the world are open to people like Vicky, ordinary people with drive and determination and passion. They are no longer the preserve of the elite mountaineers.

Whether people with money and determination, rather than the mountaineering skills and physical strength and experience built up over years of climbing, *should* be allowed in increasing numbers to try for the summit of, for example, Mount Everest, is a current and controversial question. But, for Vicky Jack, climbing the seven highest mountains in the world is about taking responsibility for her own life and raising it above the everyday and the normal. She has devoted years of careful, meticulous preparation and serious training to make sure she is fit and competent on the mountains. She has used the skills, character and gifts she has and pushed them to the farthest limits she can. For Vicky, climbing the Seven Summits has been about having fun, even when you're stuck in a tent with a man with smelly feet and you're freezing and feeling sick and don't want to climb another step. It's been about freedom and the powerful, heady joy of being in the high mountains, under the endless sky, surrounded by the beauty and grandeur of the natural world. It has always been about being, and feeling, wonderfully alive. That is the story of this book and, to Vicky, it's very simple:

If I had died on Everest, I wouldn't think it was a waste of my life. In fact, if it was possible to choose, I'd rather die on a mountain – but at the age of eighty, at the end of my life – than in an old people's home.

1

IN THE GARDEN

When she was ten Vicky Jack was given a birthday present which she has never forgotten. Her eyes still gleam with delight when she describes it, almost forty-five years later:

> It was a trapeze and Dad suspended it from a silver birch tree in the back garden. My bedroom overlooked the roof of the kitchen and washhouse and I could see over to the gooseberry bushes against the wall which separated the back garden from what we called the top garden. The top garden sloped up to the trees and, from my window, I could look out on to my trapeze. I loved it and spent hour after hour alone on it. You could use it as a swing or you could take the seat off, shorten the ropes and attach the trapeze or take away the trapeze and attach two hoops to the ropes to swing from. I remember I always used the trapeze and hoops, never the swing. When I was on the trapeze, I imagined being in the circus. It's difficult to describe the feeling. I was free! I think that's why I loved it so much.

Vicky was always happiest as a child – and, as it turned out, as an adult – when she was doing something sporty or physical in the open air – tennis, gardening, lacrosse, walking. At school in the douce Renfrewshire village of Kilmacolm where she grew up, her preferred subjects were the sciences partly because, 'in the science lab, you were moving around. I think it's the movement thing – I don't want to be sitting behind a desk.' She was Captain of Games for two years running and excelled at tennis. In fact, her dream between the ages of eleven and eighteen was to play at Wimbledon. The Jack household did not have a television until Vicky was about fifteen so she used to go to a friend's house to watch her heroes and heroines – Rod Laver, John Newcombe, Tony Roche, Billie Jean King and the elegant, dark-haired British player of the late 1960s and early 1970s, Roger Taylor, who fascinated Vicky because he used to train by running with weights strapped around his ankles. During the summer, Vicky would be on the tennis courts at the bottom of her road four or five evenings a week after supper, playing with her brother Brian or doubles with her parents or sometimes with the twins down the road, Evelyn and Gwen, who played in the Juniors at Wimbledon.

> They used to spend hours on the courts and, occasionally, I was asked to play with them. Because they played at Junior Wimbledon, I thought, 'Hey, I could do it too!' So that's how I believed my dream would be a reality.

In reality, Vicky *was* a very good tennis player – so good that a careers advisor, visiting the school, suggested that she take it up professionally. There was, of course, no question of her following this advice. As her father said, no one made money out of playing tennis. Well, not in 1971, anyway. Vicky was tickled by the whole incident.

> I remember coming home, laughing and saying to my parents, 'You'll never guess what they told me at school to do as a career!' It was more about how daft the career advisor's advice was. It was a joke, really. I was sitting six Highers!

The tennis courts belonged to St Columba's School, the private girls' school (it is mixed today) which Vicky attended from 1958 to 1971. Because the Jacks lived so near – just a hundred yards up the quiet, villa-lined Duchal Road – the school gave Vicky's father charge of a key and the family made good use of the courts whenever they were free. Today the courts are still there (converted from blaize to Astroturf), used for hockey in the winter and tennis in the summer, and at the far side beyond the fence is the Paisley and Clyde Railway Path, which used to be the railway line linking Houston, Bridge of Weir and Kilmacolm with Paisley and Glasgow. From 1869, the line carried generations of commuters and businessmen like Vicky's father the eighteen miles or so to Glasgow and back every day and, when St Columba's was opened in 1897, it was the railway which brought thousands of pupils over the years from Greenock, Bridge of Weir and beyond. The line closed in 1983 and the station, which was only a ten-minute walk from Vicky's house, was later converted into a pub and restaurant – the first pub in 'dry' Kilmacolm.

Duchal Road itself looks much the same as it did on 27 March 1953 when Vicky was born. The road is wide and quiet, the detached Victorian houses discreetly shaded and protected by trees, fences and hedges. The houses are perhaps more obviously prosperous and well-tended than back in the 1950s and 1960s. The Jacks' big red sandstone house, 'Ainslie', which her father inherited from his father, had no central heating and Vicky fondly remembers the blistered paint on the back door and the roof that leaked occasionally. The garden was shaggy and messy and rather wild – perfect for children to play in. Vicky is the youngest of the four children of Tom and Maureen Jack. Her brother Brian, who died in 1980, was two years older and her closest companion in childhood and adolescence. They shared a bedroom as young children and Vicky remembers that, if she couldn't sleep at night, Brian would give her his blankets and pillows. He was a generous, quiet boy – 'a free spirit' Vicky calls him – very like her mother and, even when Brian was older and spending time with friends of his own, he never pushed his little sister away.

> He used to take me with him to his friends if I was on my own with no one to play with or his friends would come to our house. The gang would meet in the kitchen for coffee and Mum and I would be there and they'd wander into the house in dribs and drabs. It was a nice atmosphere. They were all boys and, as they got older and got interested in girls, my job was to find them girls! Eventually, I'd say, 'Excuse me, what about me?' But they'd just laugh and say, 'Oh, no – you're one of us. You're one of the gang!'

Vicky was not so close to her sisters, Jill, six years her senior, and the eldest, Shirly, who is eight years older. The children seemed to split down the middle quite naturally and, since Jill left home when Vicky was only thirteen, the two sisters never got to know each other properly. In later life, the three sisters have all led very separate lives. Shirly's memories of growing up in Kilmacolm hardly feature Vicky at all and, as the baby of the family, Vicky's recollections are very much focused on her own little world of Mum and Dad and Brian.

She doesn't remember Shirly or Jill climbing that first Munro, Ben Bhuidhe, but they may well have since the whole family was on holiday together. They were staying in a house belonging to friends on the shores of Loch Eck, north of Dunoon, where Shirly remembers going fishing with her father. She caught her first fish – a sea trout – on Loch Eck and was particularly thrilled because, as she remembers, sea trout 'fight like hell'. Shirly also remembers her father, who was a keen fisherman, teaching her to cast on the lawn of the holiday house.

For many years in the 1960s and early 1970s, the family went to a caravan in Ardnamurchan for their summer holidays, and spent the days walking and exploring. At home in Kilmacolm, the Jacks did a good deal of walking – the obligatory Sunday afternoon walks around the local reservoir, up the local hill, Misty Law, or to Loch Thom which overlooks Greenock and Gourock and has beautiful views across to Arran. Vicky remembers walking in the woods near the golf course with Brian or her mother and then across The Moss, a watery moor teeming with birds that rose up and flapped away in great clouds when disturbed. The whirring of wings and piercing cries were magical.

At primary school she was happy and contented.

There was a lovely big playground with lots of trees. A couple of big ropes with knots hung from the trees and I remember I used to love swinging on them. And we used to play aeroplane tig and career about on roller skates. We had gardening as a subject and I excelled at this because I was the only girl who knew how to hoe! Dad had taught me. I loved gardening and used to go round at breaktime and chat with Mr McKearnan, the gardener. We'd plant lettuces and all kinds of stuff. At the end of each year at Prep School, everyone got a prize, a book for arithmetic, reading, writing etc. I'll never forget that one of the prizes I got was for gardening. All the parents were there and everyone laughed when I went up – not many people get prizes for gardening!

At home, her father grew vegetables and worked in the garden but it was because 'it had to be done, rather than because he actually enjoyed it'. Vicky enjoyed it for its own sake and because it involved physical labour. She remembers a fireman who used to get the bus from Port Glasgow to earn some extra money by gardening for the Jacks and how, one summer, she spent hours helping him to build steps up to the top garden. Her job was to scurry around the garden collecting suitable stones to use and, as the days wore on, she became more adept at eyeing up the size and dimensions and choosing the right shape of stone.

She savours this childhood memory with the intense pleasure of someone who has always taken great satisfaction in team-work and in doing a job well. Climbing the Seven Summits demanded enormous self-discipline and single-mindedness but Vicky has never been a loner. She is a rather private person who does not readily express emotions or share problems but she loves being with people, working together and solving problems. Nothing gives her greater pleasure than having a piece of work to complete or a challenge to take on – the child in the garden, diligently searching for the right stones and devoting all her energies to the task in hand, becomes the woman care-fully building her career and marshalling her resources for the challenge of climbing to the tops of high mountains.

The Jack household of Vicky's childhood was a place of phys-ical activity and doing. It was not a home where books and reading were high on the agenda. Vicky was very conscientious and able at school but the thing she hated most was having to write English essays for Monday morning – compositions she had to make up out of her head. She would always leave them to the last moment – usually the Sunday night – when her father was cleaning all the shoes for school and it could be put off no longer.

On a Sunday night, that sinking feeling set in. Often, Dad would end up more or less writing the essay for me. Mrs Jones was the English teacher and little did I know that she was perfectly well aware of what Dad did. One time I got six out of ten, with the comment, 'Tell your father it wasn't so good this week!' I'll never forget it. I showed the comment to my father – he just laughed!

Writing or reading books didn't come naturally to Vicky. She much preferred to be outdoors and freely admits that she did not read much as a child. It was partly because books were kept in a cupboard in the nursery which was very damp – the books were fusty-smelling and covered in mould and she didn't like touching them. So any notion that she may have sat for hours as a child, curled up in a chair in the library, poring over books about Everest and the high places of the world, is misplaced. She has never been an armchair traveller or a traveller whose inspiration came from childhood wonderment at dramatic stories of exploration and adventure.

But as a child she *did* want to be an explorer – or at least she had a vague sense of wanting to do something and be somewhere which was free and open and different. 'I didn't go tramping over the fields or away by myself walking all day, pretending I was an explorer. It wasn't like that. It was a state of mind, really.' So this skinny, active girl who is remembered by school friends as excelling at sports, as friendly and pleasant but having a certain reserve about her – 'quite self-contained,' says one classmate – this was a girl whose other dream, if she couldn't go to Wimbledon, was to become an explorer.

I wanted to be a marine biologist and work for *National Geographic*, which I never actually got as a periodical! I saw it in the library, I think. The interesting bit for me was to go and explore, not to read the magazine. I remember I watched *The Undersea World of Jacques Cousteau* on television at a friend's house and I liked the idea of diving in the sea, not thinking about the dangers you might meet. It was always sunny and bright in my mind and you'd see all these beautiful fish and explore the ocean. I thought that would be brilliant.

For someone who has carved out such a successful career for herself, Vicky seems to have been gloriously unconcerned all along the way about *details*. What excites her are grand ideas and seemingly impossible challenges. Once the idea has grabbed her, only then does she direct her huge capacity for hard work and meticulous planning towards realising her dreams. These two sides to her character – a delight in a challenge and a powerful ability to achieve specific goals – have brought her considerable career success and enabled her to take on the hugely demanding – and serious – task of climbing the Seven Summits. These qualities are evident in her childhood and while she was growing up. She set herself very high standards at school and loved biology, chemistry and physics. Although she was consistently in the top third throughout her senior years, work was a constant worry.

> I took school quite seriously and I do remember having this great weight on my shoulders about work. There was an angst there. I always wanted to be top of the class. Occasionally I'd get top marks and I'd think, 'Yes!' But then I'd be back again in the top third. But I wanted to be top.

She was surprised and thrilled when she was made Games Captain and enormously proud of all the little colours for sporting achievement which she sewed on to her gym tunic each year. There are many photographs of Vicky in the school magazines over the years: Lacrosse First team, 1967–68, 1968–69, 1970–71; Tennis team 1969–70, 1970–71; Prefects 1969–70. In all the photographs, she looks happy and relaxed, with a big wide smile, and her long blond hair is pulled into the obligatory hairstyle of generations of sporty schoolgirls – enormous bunches tied with elastic bands. Her name is also on a prize-winners' plaque at the main school entrance – the Fiona Keydon Memorial Prize (1970–71) for outstanding service to the school. Her games teacher, Mrs Sandeman, says Vicky 'was always a very reliable sort of girl both on and off the sports field. She would never let you down.'

There is no doubt that Vicky was a successful all-rounder

at school but her academic achievements were sometimes at the expense of an unrelenting self-imposed pressure to succeed and almost crippling anxiety when it came to exams.

I found exams really difficult. I got really worked up and swotted and swotted for them. I remember Mum getting really worried because I was absolutely ashen for days and weeks and she would force me to go out for walks. So I developed a very strict regime. I would study, study, study and then think, 'Oh, no, I've got to take an hour to go out and walk.' Or, 'Oh, no, I've got to take half an hour to eat.' I took exams far too seriously.

It's tempting to wonder which aspects of her personality Vicky inherited from or shared with her parents. They were a contrasting couple. Her father, Tom Jack, owned and ran a children's clothing manufacturing business at 128 Ingram Street in Glasgow. He and his younger brother, Donald, inherited the business from their father. Thomas Jack and Company Ltd made children's clothes under the label 'Agatha' and sold to outlets such as Harrods and House of Fraser. Each morning, Vicky's father boarded the train at Kilmacolm, along with all the other fathers and businessmen, spent the day at the factory and came back on the same train every evening. In the summer, Brian and Vicky would run to the station in the evening sun and sit on the platform bench, waiting for their father's train to arrive. Vicky speaks of her father, who died in 1989, with great affection and considerable understanding. He was a complex man who took the responsibilities of fatherhood very seriously.

From what I have been told, Dad was very wild before he got married but, once he married Mum, he took the responsibility of being a husband and father very much to heart. As a father, he was sometimes strict but always kind. He worked very hard because he was terribly concerned about providing for us but the business was never a great moneymaker and he was never well off. I think that worried him. There was a tension about my father. He was very tall and straight, always polite and gentlemanly. I know some people found him quite formal and perhaps sometimes a little aloof but I never did.

By contrast, Maureen Jack – sixteen years younger than her husband – was what Vicky describes as 'a free spirit', someone utterly unconcerned with and, in all probability, blissfully unaware of social pressures or convention. Later in life, after the family had all grown up, Maureen was persuaded by a friend to go along to an art class in the village. She discovered a considerable talent for painting, mostly in watercolours and gouache. Sheila Fraser was a close friend and she, too, joined the art class. For the first lesson, she remembers, they all went to Maureen's house and ended up painting the dustbin because 'that just happened to be what we were looking at!' They often went to friends' gardens to paint and Sheila was put in charge of getting permission to hold the classes in the big, secluded gardens all over Kilmacolm. She says Maureen 'was just a natural. She didn't believe she could do anything but she was naturally talented at painting.'

Elspeth MacRobert is another friend. On the wall of her living room, there is a lovely, delicate watercolour Maureen painted of Knapps Loch, a beautiful lochan nestled among the green slopes just on the edge of Kilmacolm. Elspeth remembers Maureen with almost fierce affection, describing her as 'extremely shy and very, very quiet', a lovely woman with fair hair and a nice figure who 'was probably a bomb when she was in the Wrens!' Maureen, like most married women of that generation, didn't go out to work and Elspeth remembers she used to bring along first Brian and then Vicky when they went for coffee in the village. Looking after the children, meeting friends and running the house were the main occupations for Maureen although Vicky remembers that her mother was not particularly interested in domestic chores.

> She hated cooking and she wasn't a particularly good cook. We used to love her lentil soup, though. We had a lady who came and cleaned the house downstairs while Mum did the upstairs. I don't really know how she spent her days because I, of course, was at school. But I do remember she occasionally went for a 'rest' in the afternoons – she suffered a bit from headaches. When she was in the Wrens, she was part of the gymnastics team and she enjoyed hillwalking and played tennis. I was extremely close to both my parents and loved them deeply. I knew that their love for me was unconditional and that always gave me great strength and purpose in life.

Vicky was particularly close to her mother and looked after her for many years after Tom Jack died, when she was living alone in the cottage in Balquhidder which she and her husband moved to in 1975. Vicky visited Maureen nearly every weekend even though her career meant she was living and working far away in Aviemore, Aberdeen and Inverness and travelling all over the world to climb. They enjoyed each other's company immensely and Vicky describes her as 'my best friend'. Her older sister, Shirly, had a much more difficult relationship with her mother. 'We didn't really communicate very well,' she says. The sense of freedom about Maureen, the quiet moving through life which Vicky found so attractive, was experienced by her sister as a lack of energy and will. Shirly was the eldest child of whom much was expected and she admits that she gave her parents a hard time as a teenager. During the years when she rebelled against what she describes as her father's 'Victorian' strictness, she wanted her mother to be on her side and stand up for her – something she felt she did not do.

Vicky and her mother had a very special bond, a closeness in which some shared attitude to life and living, some view of the world, drew them firmly together. Perhaps, too, Vicky enjoyed that more relaxed, less pressured position of the youngest child. She also enjoyed a closer relationship with her father than any of her siblings.

I remember when I was about twenty and Dad was trying to sell the house. He was standing on the front door step with the prospective buyer and I was late to catch a train into Glasgow. I remember running out of the house, seeing him standing there, feeling awkward that he was talking to someone else and not wanting to run through the two of them because that was bad manners. I raced up to Dad, gave him a big hug and said, 'See you later.' Later on, Mum told me that that had meant a huge amount to Dad and the stranger, apparently, had said, 'I wish my daughters would do that to me.' That display of affection broke a barrier with Dad. I'm not going to say that after that we were very close because I think we were close before that. I used to sit on the floor and lean against Dad's leg when he was sitting in front of the fire. He would stroke my hair and I loved that. So I think there was that bond but I didn't pour my heart out to him.

The talking was all done with her mother – although Vicky jokes that she's 'still waiting to be told the facts of life!' Activities and outings were organised by her father. Shirly remembers it was their father who introduced them all to sports and hill-walking and fishing. And Vicky certainly inherited her father's powerful work ethic, perhaps even that self-imposed pressure to succeed and achieve. Shirly, with a sister's eye for detail, describes Vicky's ambition and drive as 'turbo-charged. She's fiercely focused. I think she could do with slowing down a bit and relaxing. She knows that.' They have different outlooks on life but what they do share is vivid memories of something which helped to shape how Vicky thought about work and career – their father's clothing business.

As a child of about five, Vicky – with her pretty blond hair and blue eyes – modelled some of the 'Agatha' line for the catalogues.

> It was always hugely exciting going to Dad's factory, along a dirty, cobbled alley, through the doorway and into the big, clunking lift with the heavy metal gate. Then up past S. & P. Harris who made shirts and out into a stone stairwell, through a tall wooden door into a corridor of brown linoleum.

Tom Jack's office was at the far end of the corridor and Vicky remembers it with astonishing clarity – the brown linoleum floor, the huge window and, below it, a big, deep shelf full of files and, in front of that, her father's huge wooden desk, chipped and worn, with a leather top. Behind the desk was a chair with a large cushion on it, covering the hole where the seat had fallen through. On top of the desk sat a phone with a brown speaker box beside it, a few pieces of paper and not much else. Tom Jack was a neat man.

Vicky vividly remembers the sights, sounds and smells of the factory: the hollow sound of her footsteps on the linoleum, echoing to the high ceilings; the chemical smell of the treatments used on the fabrics which sat in huge bales in the stockroom; the pockmarks gouged by years of high-heeled shoes on the wooden floor in the machine room where between forty and sixty women worked; the *zip-zip-zip* of the massed sewing machines; the *clack-clack* of the fabric cutters working on the laying-up tables; and the rhythmic *thump-pshhh-thump-pshhh* from the big steam irons as finished garments were noisily pressed, ready for the delivery rail. This was a magical, thrilling world for Vicky – a world of ceaseless activity, of camaraderie and banter, of hard, manual work and long hours. Shirly loved the fabrics and materials. She had taught herself to make clothes on her mother's Singer sewing machine, first for her dolls, later as experiments for Brian (lucky boy!) and then for herself, and she adored coming to the factory where her father let her pick little bits of fabric from what seemed to her an Aladdin's cave of colours and textures.

Between the ages of about sixteen and eighteen, Vicky worked in the factory during holidays and over the summer but, as a child, her principal memories are of being led through the factory floor by the designer, Miss Lucia Maxwell, who wore miniskirts, black high-heeled boots and a lot of mascara and lipstick and whose favourite colour was sweetie pink. Vicky would be paraded round the factory in Miss Maxwell's very pink designs and then taken to a nearby studio for the photographing.

The other abiding memory is of the times, twice a year, when Tom Jack introduced the new range of designs. There was tremendous angst during those periods – it required a huge amount of time to write out all the sample tickets for each new line and there was always pressure for a new range to sell well. Each ticket had the code number, size and colour range and it was all done manually. The great thrill for Vicky was when her father brought tickets home with him to work on and everyone would help out. She would be given a big sheet of paper, one per style, and a bunch of tickets. She would then write each ticket out very carefully, taking the numbers and codes off the big sheet, bind them into a neat bundle and give them to her father, ready for the next lot. Like helping the gardener build a wall in the top garden, here was a task ideally suited to Vicky's love of organising and her delight in working in a team. That's why she remembers it so vividly.

Looking back on childhood, I liked to be with people and to feel as if I was helping. I like having company and all these little scenarios from childhood are linked to doing things with people – as a team. And, when it comes to climbing, the joy for me is sharing experiences with others, more than getting to the top.

Getting to the top *does* matter a great deal though, however much enjoyment there is in being part of a team. It matters enough that Vicky spent six years fulfilling her ambition to get to the top of the Seven Summits. She enjoyed it all immensely but she also took the challenge very seriously. American businessman Bob Jen climbed Mount Everest with Vicky on her second attempt. He believes that teamwork will only get you so far, on that mountain at least, as 'by the time you get to the South Col at 26,000 feet, you're on your own'. At that altitude, when your body is dying, cell by cell, from lack of oxygen and the summit is still three thousand feet above you, it is your own willpower and desire that will get you there.

At eighteen, Vicky Jack did not know that thirty-three years later she would be standing on the summit of Mount Everest. All she knew was that she had good Higher results, a place at Stirling University and she was going there to study first biology and then marine biology. After that, off she would go to work for *National Geographic* and explore the world. But then her father told her the bad news – he could not afford to send her to university. The business was not doing well enough and Vicky did not qualify for a grant so that was it. None of her siblings had gone to university – none of them had wanted to – but it was still rather a shock to have her plans upset. The big idea – her *only* idea for her future, actually – had evaporated. Although she was secretly rather relieved at the thought of not having to study and sit exams for the next few years, another anxiety began to simmer. It was the question which was to dog Vicky from now on, after each career challenge had been overcome and each goal achieved – 'What do I do now?'

2

TRAVELLING

There is a story Vicky tells about herself in primary school which reveals something rather delightful about her personality, even though she was only seven when it happened.

One day, I was in the cloakroom and, on the bench underneath my coat peg, I found a box of 'Joy' biscuits. I will never forget them. They were individually wrapped chocolate biscuits with a filling, rather like caramel wafers. I thought, 'Oh, someone's left me a gift!' I checked and asked if anyone else had a present on their bench but no one had, only me. So I shared them round and we were all happily munching them when in came the headmistress, who asked if we'd seen a box of 'Joy' biscuits. I said yes and she explained that one of the girls at school had mistakenly brought the box from home – her mother had meant her to take only one biscuit for break – and she asked where it was. I said, 'Well, it was under my peg and I thought it was a present for me. We've shared them round and we've eaten them all.' So the teacher took me to one side and gently explained that, if something which is rather nice arrives unexpectedly, don't automatically assume that it's a present. She said you should always check where it's come from and why it's arrived before you eat it. I remember feeling awful then but it had never occurred to me for an instant that the biscuits belonged to someone else and that it had been a mistake. As far as I was concerned, the fairies had left me a rather nice present!

It's just a story from childhood but, like so many vividly preserved moments from our mysterious early years, it captures something powerful and it speaks of a kind of happy hopefulness about Vicky which does seem to run through her life. 'Climbing the seven highest mountains across the continents – I don't know anything about them but it sounds like fun, I'll do it!' That seems a far cry from assuming that a box of biscuits left on a bench are a gift from the fairies but, in a funny, human way, it's not – both responses come from a streak of naive spontaneity which has been part of Vicky's personality since childhood. Perhaps it's simply that caramel biscuits and mountains tend to bring it out most naturally.

When her plans to study marine biology at Stirling University collapsed, Vicky had no idea what to do instead. Then, out of the blue, a family she babysat for in the village phoned. They had some friends in America, the Wilburs, who needed an au pair – would Vicky like the job for a year? Vicky was thrilled and immediately said she would love to go and, three or four weeks later, in September 1971, her parents saw her off on the plane at Prestwick airport. By that time, of course, excitement had turned to apprehension – here she was at eighteen, never been away from home before, never been on an aeroplane, never been out of Scotland, and, for the next year, she would be living with a strange family, thousands of miles away and looking after two young children.

It turned out to be a wonderful year. Southport is an area in the coastal town of Fairfield, Connecticut, on Long Island Sound, sixty miles north of New York. It was – and is – a predominantly white and upper-middle-class family area of beautiful white clapboard houses, broad tree-lined avenues, safe, pretty streets and prosperous historically preserved neighbourhoods and, in the harbour, there are dozens of sailing yachts and cruisers. 'The Kilmacolm of Fairfield' is how Laura Wilbur describes it. Laura had gone to St Columba's School in Kilmacolm and her mother knew of Vicky's family. Her husband, Packer, grew up in Southport and, when he met Laura, they settled in his home town to raise a family. When Vicky arrived, she was to look after five-year-old Alison and Andrew who was about eighteen months. A few months before the end of the year Laura had her third child, Gillie.

The Wilburs were tremendously kind to me. First of all they bought me a bicycle and then, realising that wasn't very useful for ferrying the children around, they taught me to drive. I got my licence and they gave me an old Ford Mustang as my car. I had a ball that year. Occasionally, I went to the Congregational church with the family and got to know all their friends. Packer Wilbur worked tremendously long hours on Wall Street and, at weekends, he used to unwind by going to the local hardware store. He loved gadgets and occasionally he'd take me along as well, for an outing. We used to buy doughnuts first and then eat them as we wandered around the store. It was great fun.

When she wasn't eating doughnuts, Vicky looked after the children, helped with birthday parties and playgroups, drove Alison to nursery school, carved pumpkins for Halloween and travelled with the family on holiday to South Carolina and to Antigua in the West Indies. She also travelled on her own around the East Coast and visited New York City, Philadelphia and Boston. In fact, she enjoyed herself so much that year that, when Packer Wilbur suggested that she should stay on in America and try to get into Harvard, Vicky jumped at the chance. But, when she wrote to tell her parents of her great new idea, they were not happy. They didn't want her to take such a big step on her own when she was thousands of miles away. She was to come home.

Vicky accepted the decision with a good grace and came back, happy to see her parents again, but, after a while, she began to feel aimless and frustrated. It had been a fantastic year abroad and her horizons had seemed limitless but, now that she was back, she felt she had not made any progress and it was all a bit of an anti-climax. She was nineteen and living at home while most of her school friends had moved on and she still had no career in mind. She desperately needed something to aim for.

Over the next year, she moved around, trying different jobs. She started a business studies course at Reid Kerr College in Paisley but left after a few months and went to a typing school in Johnston to learn touch-typing. It was a rather bizarre experience since the 'office' was actually a shop window and passers-by could look in at the girls as they were learning to type. It ended mercifully and abruptly when the teacher put her arm round Vicky's shoulder after a few weeks and told her, pityingly, 'You'll never be a typist, dear.' Vicky then spent some months in London, living with her sister, Jill, and working for a company called OCL – Overseas Containers Limited – first in the personnel office and then in the export trade department.

Eventually, no further forward in her career plans, she came back to Scotland and worked in the fabric stockroom of her father's factory, where she was responsible for lifting bales of material from the shelves and loading them on to a machine like an enormous toilet-roll holder.

I have a very vivid memory of the smell in the fabric room. It was from the finishing they put on the fabrics, especially on the corduroy – a strong chemical smell mixed with the smell of the material and of the brown paper it was all wrapped up in.

She would measure out the different lengths for the different orders – at that time, in the early 1970s, corduroy was all the rage – and take them to the ladies at the laying-up tables for cutting. Often she would help with the laying-up and cutting as well, which the women loved because they were on piece work and any extra help meant they produced more and so got paid more. Vicky loved the work, loved the energising atmosphere, the busyness of the production line and the friendly banter of the women. With hindsight, she thinks she might have enjoyed, as she says, 'having a crack at running the business' but, back then, she had no thoughts of working for her father. Tom Jack bought threads from J. & P. Coats in Paisley and, one day, he suggested that Vicky should apply for a job with the company. She did and was offered one of the first two places in a brand-new management training scheme for women which Coats had introduced.

Vicky has an old newspaper cutting from 1974 headlined 'Two Girls in a Man's World'. Above the text is a wonderfully posed photograph of Vicky in a checked miniskirt, sitting back to back with the other trainee, Anne Armstrong, on some kind of bollard in Carnaby Street in London. Blond and brunette are both beaming confidently at the camera. 'Two Scots girls are on their way to the top in a man's world,' the story begins, 'chosen for a two-year grooming course, until now reserved exclusively for men. When it is over, top jobs will be open to them, even those on managerial level.' The article goes on to describe the different areas of the business that the girls will learn about and ends with a comment from a Coats spokesman about what will happen at the end of the two years. 'They will have seen all facets of our business. Then they will pick where their future lies.'

Picking out her future was, unfortunately, Vicky's problem. Much as she enjoyed the course, travelling around the country learning about the business and having fun, she simply could not bear to choose an area to specialise in. She felt unable to make what she thought would be a life-binding decision, at twenty-two years of age, about whether she wanted to go into finance or manufacturing or sales or any other area of the business. In the end, she couldn't make the choice and, still unsure of what to do, she decided to travel.

So off she went to Europe and, for the next year or so, put off any decisions about her future until she could somehow find that elusive purpose she was looking for. She had earned some money on the training scheme and so she eked out her savings, living on very little. 'I'm good at that,' she says. She slept on beaches and in youth hostels. While she was in Switzerland she slept in the grounds of a clock factory in Geneva and was taken in by a minister's family for a few days. One night she slept in the woods in Chamonix and, at other times, she would meet people on the road and they would journey together for a few days.

She travelled southwards, to Greece, to see her brother, Brian. The lovely, gentle boy who had been Vicky's soulmate in childhood had lost his way during his teenage years, got into bad company at boarding school and had eventually left Scotland and gone travelling. To the great despair and unhappiness of his family, he was arrested and imprisoned in Greece for possession of drugs. These were troubling times for Vicky, who was so close to her brother, and for her parents, separated from their son and unable to help him. She visited him several times while she was travelling, first in Athens and then in Crete, where he had been sent to an open prison. The hardship for Brian and the pain for Vicky of seeing her beloved brother in these circumstances can only be imagined. Such griefs are too private and shattering to speak about and they are never erased. It was to be the last time Vicky saw her brother, who died five years later in Amsterdam in 1980.

Eventually she made her way back to Scotland where her parents welcomed her, as ever, with open arms. She was no further forward, however, and at twenty-three she still had no idea what she wanted to do with her life. Then a man from the past walked back into her life at Christmas time as she was kneeling on the floor of the toy department in Frasers store in Glasgow. She was on the floor because she was playing a game.

She was playing a game because she had a temporary job in Frasers and she reckoned she could sell the toys and games better if she had a go herself. There she was, engrossed in her game, surrounded by overheated shoppers and tinsel and festive decorations, when in walked David Miller, the personnel director from Coats whom she had met while on the training scheme. He was buying Christmas presents for his children and, after watching her for a minute, he strode up and said, 'Come back to Coats and I'll wipe that smile off your face. You're having too much fun down there!'

Vicky gave the matter not a second's thought and said, 'OK.'

David, who is now retired from Coats, recalls that Vicky seemed to him to be in a dead-end job and he felt she could do better. 'We'd been rather impressed with her on the trainee scheme,' he said. 'She was always highly presentable, competent and straightforward.' He had no hesitation in offering her the chance to start again.

For her part, Vicky says she accepted his offer simply because she knew she had to start her career sometime.

> I didn't have a grand career plan at all at that stage and I really needed a goal and something to drive me. Frasers offered me a management training scheme but I didn't fancy retail. So I thought, 'OK, I'll go back to Coats.' But I'm sure David Miller was thinking to himself, 'Where on earth am I going to put her?'

Vicky had no training to her credit so David, with delightful logic and irony, put her to work on the very apprenticeship scheme she had abandoned two years earlier and told her to improve it because there had been such a high drop-out rate. That was her first proper job and the first of fifteen years she was to spend at Coats, from 1976 to 1991. Through the encouragement of David Miller, she also became involved in voluntary work. She was asked to be a governor of Outward

Bound at Loch Eil and David recalls that, at one of the first meetings she attended, there was a lecture by Reinhold Messner, the first man to climb Everest solo without oxygen.

However, despite being successful and busy in the Coats job, working in an office was never enough for Vicky. There was always, as there had been at school, that weight on her shoulders – the feeling that she was not doing what came most naturally. What came most naturally was to be outdoors, on the move, free, pushing herself to the limit. It was time to start climbing hills.

*   *   *   *   *

Glen Shiel in Ross and Cromarty is a rugged and beautiful West Highland glen which boasts some of the most soaring and impressive mountain scenery in Scotland. The glen stretches for ten miles from Glen Cluanie in the east to the head of Loch Duaich at Shiel Bridge in the west. Keep travelling west through Loch Duaich and Loch Alsh and you reach the Isle of Skye at Kyle of Lochalsh. To the north of Glen Shiel the famous Five Sisters of Kintail soar upwards in a heaped mass and, on the south side of the glen, a continuous chain of mountains shoulders its way dramatically through the landscape for over nine miles.

On 10 June 1719, some years after the failure of the 1715 Jacobite Rising, the Battle of Glen Shiel was fought here as part of another attempt to regain the throne for the Stuarts. The Jacobite army was joined by around 300 Spaniards but the mixed force was defeated by the Hanoverian troops and, once more, the Jacobite leaders were forced to flee. On the north side of the glen, there is a hill named in honour of the Spanish soldiers – Sgurr nan Spainteach, 'Peak of the Spaniards'.

Some fifty-four years after the Battle of Glen Shiel was fought, Dr Johnson and his trusty companion James Boswell traversed the glen on horseback. Nearly two centuries after that Vicky Jack came to the glen to tackle one of the best extended high-level ridges in the Highlands – the South Glen Shiel Ridge. This ridge includes no fewer than seven Munros, all spread out in a single line along the southern side of the glen. Once you climb the first hill at the east end, Creag a' Mhaim, 'Rock of the Big Rounded Hill', you continue along the ridge at an average height of at least 2,600 feet for nearly nine miles. The scenery is breathtaking and the names of the other six Munros gloriously conjure up the wild beauty of the area: Druim Shionnach, 'Ridge of the Foxes'; Aonach air Chrith, 'Ridge of Trembling'; Maol Chinn-dearg, 'Bald Red Hill'; Sgurr an Doire Leathain, 'Peak of the Broad Oak Grove'; Sgurr an Lochain, 'Peak of the Little Loch'; and the western summit, Creag nan Damh, 'Rock of the Stags'.

Most guide books suggest that the walker splits the seven Munros into the eastern four and western three and tackles them over two days. That thought never occurred to Vicky when she set off from the Cluanie Inn in the early morning of 23 July 1988 – fit hillwalkers 'bag' seven Munros in one go by tackling the South Glen Shiel Ridge in a day and so would she. Because you are on a ridge you are not climbing up and down seven mountains but it is still hard going and demands stamina and strength to keep going for a very long day. Vicky revelled in it. She had started hill-climbing a couple of years before-hand because she wanted to get to know Scotland beyond the roads. She had friends from England who would come and visit her and she realised that her knowledge of the hills and lochs and interior landscape of her native country was distinctly lacking. So she began to hillwalk – she remembers she used to drag every unsuspecting visitor up Ben Lomond, whatever the weather – and she had several Munros to her credit by the time she had been working at Coats for a couple of years. When a boyfriend asked her to do the South Glen Shiel Ridge and she realised, at the end of the day, that she now had seven more Munros under her belt, that was when she began to take the idea of 'Munro-bagging' seriously. 'Seven Munros in one day!

I thought, "I can do this!" That day got me hooked on hill-walking and hooked on Munros. It was something to go for.'

Sir Hugh Munro, an Englishman by birth and a co-founder of the Scottish Mountaineering Club, was the first person to compile a list of those separate Scottish mountains over 3,000 feet (914 metres). His original 'Munro Tables' classification, published in the *Scottish Mountaineering Club Journal* in 1891, identified 236 hills but, over the decades, more modern and improved surveying techniques have revised the list several times and, since 1997, the agreed number has stood at 284. When Vicky climbed her final one in 1996, there were 277 recognised Munros and it took her almost ten years to complete them (she climbed the extra ones very soon afterwards). It was that day in Glen Shiel which gave her the greatest spur to take this on as a serious challenge.

Hillwalking – and racing sailing on the Firth of Clyde, which she took up in 1990 – kept Vicky sane and happy in the years of career building. In her fifteen years with Coats, she worked her way up in the personnel department to become personnel manager and it was tough, slogging work in a company not known for promoting women to its top jobs. Much of her work in the late 1980s had involved closing down companies all over the country which were owned by Coats and the constant pressure meant that getting out to the hills or on to the water became an indispensable release. But she could not bring herself to go walking simply for relaxation. She had to have a purpose and the purpose was to climb all the Munros. The index at the back of her Munro book is covered with her tiny handwriting in black biro. Each Munro has a date opposite it, noting when she climbed it, with the occasional comment like 'second time' or 'and again' which means simply that she climbed some of them more than once. At the top of one page, there is the date '2/9/91' and the comment 'halfway there!'

She took every opportunity to go up a Munro. Her parents

had moved from Kilmacolm in 1975 to the cottage in Balquhidder where Vicky now lives. Her father had also become ill with cancer and Vicky spent a great deal of her time visiting her parents and helping to support her mother as her father became increasingly weak. When her mother had to go in to hospital in Stirling for an operation, her father was admitted to a cottage hospital in Crieff and Vicky's weekends and evenings were spent driving between Stirling, Crieff and work in Glasgow. Anyone else might have been pleased just to get through the day and collapse in front of the television but not Vicky.

It shows you how much the outdoors matters to me. I remember visiting Mum in hospital in Stirling, then belting up the road to pick something up at the cottage in Balquhidder, then going round to Crieff to see Dad. And, on my way, I stopped and went up Ben Chonzie, a Munro just outside Crieff. I virtually ran up the hill because it's quite a long approach and I knew I had to get down in time to see Dad during visiting hours. I really pushed myself up that hill but I absolutely needed it to balance all the other pressures in my life.

When Maureen came out of hospital, she was unable to look after her husband on her own so Tom went into long-term hospital care in Stirling. He was in a small ward for about a year until his death in 1989. Vicky continued to look after her mother and visit at weekends, despite Maureen's protests that she shouldn't be spending so much time there. It never entered Vicky's head *not* to be there.

During those years of serious hillwalking, it is difficult to work out how Vicky had time to do the ordinary, laborious tasks in life like cleaning the toilet or doing the shopping or putting on a washing. Every minute of every day and weekend seems to have been taken up by work, visiting her parents, sailing or climbing Munros.

In 1991, she left Coats and joined the offshore fabrication division of Trafalgar House as a human resources manager, based first in Edinburgh and then in Aberdeen. A typical weekend went something like this:

> Quite often, on a Friday evening, I would drive to somewhere straight from Aberdeen – often right across to the west coast. I'd arrive about 10 o'clock at night at wherever I was staying, absolutely shattered from the week's work – I might have been in London, Teesside or elsewhere through the week. Then, on Saturday morning, we'd be setting out for the hill at 7 a.m. and I'd drive back to Aberdeen on the Sunday night, having done hills on the Sunday as well. Monday was always a tough day!

Why do it? Why push yourself so hard, both physically and mentally? Vicky's answer is not complicated or particularly profound. It is the feeling of release and of freedom. 'As soon as I get up high in the hills, everything lifts,' she says. She hates starting in the rain and sometimes it's a real effort to push herself up when her mind is full of work issues and everyday worries and she feels tired and stressed. But she keeps going because she craves the exhilaration and delight of being revived and washed through by high places. And then there are the glorious summer days on the Scottish hills, when the air is warm and the wind carries the scent of grass and the sky is duck-egg blue; a big bee buzzes lazily past and, somewhere high, high above, a skylark pours out endless, sweet music. These are days like no others.

Vicky does not like to describe herself as a technical climber but she is certainly able and experienced on the hills. Tackling the Seven Summits meant she had to become proficient in certain techniques and in using essential climbing equipment, such as crampons, ice axes, karabiners (a special metal clip), ropes, knots and jumars (a mechanical device for ascending a rope). The Munros can all be climbed without any special mountaineering skills or equipment, with the exception of Sgurr Dearg on Skye with its Inaccessible Pinnacle, a towering, pointed slab of rock which is embedded in the steepest side of the mountain. Sgurr Dearg is part of the Cuillin Ridge and climbing those Munros was the only occasion when Vicky can remember having to overcome fear. She was with a group being guided by the well-known Cuillin guide, Gerry Ackroyd.

We didn't do the whole Cuillin ridge from start to finish without stopping as it includes several Munros and they're very pointy and steep. You're scrambling on rock and scree and you need ropes and a head for heights which I don't really have. I'll never forget going across one of the ridges that was so narrow we sat with a leg on either side and had to haul ourselves along. Gerry, our guide, went across easily and turned to us. 'Right, who's first?' Everyone hung back so I said, 'All right, I'll go.' I was taking my time getting into position, straddling the ridge and trying to calm my nerves and Gerry shouted, 'For goodness sake, hurry up! Why are you hanging about?'

When I'm scared I can become rather flippant and, without thinking, I shouted back to him, 'Well, my mother wouldn't approve of this.'

'Why not?' he yelled back.

'She always told me to keep my legs together!'

Everyone laughed and it eased the tension, which made it much easier to get across that scary ridge.

Vicky did the Munros most often with one or two other people. When she went up alone, it was usually in the summer and on the easier ascents. For many years, she went up hills with Jean Davie and Shona Armstrong who are both GPs. Jean has known Vicky since they shared a flat in Edinburgh for a while in the early 1990s. She has been up many Munros with Vicky and says of her friend, 'Well, she was quite focused about it and I would say, if you went up a hill with Vicky, you'd have quite a high chance of getting to the top! She wasn't like some people who get tired and give up a few hundred feet from the summit.' Hillwalking with Vicky was strenuous. 'She always did more talking than anyone else on the way up because she was fitter,' Jean says but it was always enjoyable. As they climbed, they used to talk a lot about life, family, career, friends, relationships.

I think Vicky's more relaxed up a hill. She talks about things when she's up a hill – not really on the first hill but more on the second and the third and the longer you were out for, the more she would talk about what was going on in her life at the time. She's a good friend when you're going up a hill. Maybe, if you were having a bad relationship, you could talk it through with her and she'd give you surprisingly good advice. You would know that probably she knew what she was talking about!

Occasionally Jean and Vicky got lost – once, memorably, on Cairngorm when the weather closed in and they ended up going round in circles, eventually coming off the hill on the wrong side and having to plod twelve weary miles back to the car. Although Vicky's friends knew that she was trying to climb all the Munros, it wasn't something she talked about constantly. And, even when she was training for the Seven Summits, she was still the same old Vicky – good company and relaxed on the hills. At least, Jean recalls with a laugh, until she started packing her rucksack with telephone directories when she was training for Mount McKinley.

It was unbelievable! I used to go on the hills with her when she was carrying them and it was only then that I could go at the same rate as her! We went along the South Glen Shiel Ridge once with another friend and Vicky obviously had too many phone books. That was the only time I can remember she looked as if she was struggling. She 'redistributed' them twice and Shona and I got some each. And she actually asked for a rest on the way down which is very un-Vicky like!

Shona has known Vicky for more than fifteen years and has climbed some difficult and demanding Munros with her. She will never forget the day in November 1995 when she, Vicky, Jean Davie and Vicky's sister, Shirly, set off to climb three of the Cairngorms – Carn a' Mhaim, Ben Macdui and Derry Cairngorm. It was a four-and-a-half mile walk-in before they reached the hills. They got to the top of Carn a' Mhaim, made a long descent and kept going on the hard slog to the summit of Ben Macdui. By mid afternoon a thick peasouper had blanketed the hills and for an hour they trudged on. Gradually they realised the lie of the land was wrong and they had missed their course. So they all agreed to backtrack and fortunately, by sheer chance, hit a path which they followed down to Loch Etchachan, in the pitch black, with no torches, all of them bitterly cold. From there they had a three-hour walk back to the car, which they reached, exhausted, at 9 p.m. 'And we ran out of petrol, too!' Shona remembers. 'But eventually we limped into Ballater. We were very, very lucky. After that, I made myself go on a navigation course because being lost for that hour or so had frightened me so badly.'

But the glorious days on the hills with Vicky outnumbered the scary ones. The following year, on a gleaming August day, Shona and Vicky and another friend walked from the Linn of Dee over four Munros – the Devil's Point, Cairn Toul, Angel's Peak and Braeriach. It took them twelve hours, above 4,000 feet the whole way, and Shona loved every minute. 'It was a marvellous, marvellous day. One of the best walks I've ever done.'

In these years of Munro-climbing with friends and on her own, as her career became more demanding, Vicky pushed herself harder and harder both at work and out on the hills.

Her father died before she moved to Trafalgar House so he never knew that she was made a director in an intensely competitive and male-dominated company. He did not live to see his daughter complete the Munros or become the first Scotswoman to climb the Seven Summits and the oldest British woman to get to the top of Everest. He had sometimes reacted with a rather underplayed, Scottish reserve to her drive and success. Vicky remembers the day in the living room at Balquhidder when she told her parents that she had been made chair of the Glasgow Council for Voluntary Service. 'Dad made some flippant comment – which he did when he felt awkward – and I remember feeling very upset that he hadn't genuinely congratulated me or said, "Well done!"' But it was awkwardness, not unkindness, and there was never any rancour between father and daughter.

Vicky always loved him deeply and feels she understands him more as she grows older herself. Old photographs show how very like her father she is physically – he was tall and lean, wiry and fit looking, with a shy smile and a clear gaze. They shared a hillwalker's build. Her father had a great love for the outdoors and it was he who encouraged the children to enjoy the hills. Vicky has never lost that childhood thrill of running up Ben Buidhe with her brother, Brian, desperate to get to the top and wanting to get down quickly again. She still runs down hills, when she is on her own, from sheer exhilaration – just like a child.

In the index to her Munro book she has written the date 4/8/96 opposite A'Mhaighdean ('The Maiden'), the remote and majestic hill away up in the north-west of Scotland. More importantly, beside it is the cheerful little comment in black ink, 'Only 1 more to go!' Just under two months later, all the effort of the last ten years of hillwalking would be finally rewarded, as just one Munro remained.

3

THE HIGHEST HILL IN EUROPE
MOUNT ELBRUS

It was the afternoon of 28 September 1996 and Vicky was standing in the driving rain on the summit of Slioch, high above Loch Maree in the far north-west of Scotland. She had done it – 277 Munros successfully climbed. It was the culmination of ten years of tramping up hills across Scotland, in all weathers, at weekends, on summer evenings and snatched afternoons, after long days at the office in a life bursting at the seams with demanding work and physically demanding play.

A couple of months earlier, she had started a new job as human resources director of North of Scotland Water Authority. NOSWA had been created in April 1995 out of three regional and three island authorities and Vicky was responsible for bringing in new systems for recruitment, pay, grading, job evaluation and a whole raft of other areas. Coming from the private sector into a public sector body, she was there to develop and introduce new practices into this freshly created organisation and to negotiate with unions in order to get it done. It was to prove as challenging and consuming as the job she had just left at Trafalgar House.

At Trafalgar House she had been very much a lone woman working in a man's world. The offshore oil and gas division of which she was HR director was a huge organisation with massive fabrication yards in Methil in Fife and on Teesside and a pipework company in Stockton-on-Tees. Engineers, scaffolders, welders, electricians, these were the men Vicky was working with and had to be responsible for, as well as office staff, site workers, union representatives – in all, up to 8,000 people across the division. She would go into these enormous yards with their towering sheds, challenged by the realisation of the size of the job. She knew that some of these men were looking at her and thinking, 'What's this woman doing here?' And Vicky was thinking, in the early days as she learned the ropes of an industry which was totally new to her, 'What do I know? I've come from a company that makes thread!' It was a steep learning curve, a full-on, demanding world of people, politics and a multimillion pound industry.

She was extremely successful at Trafalgar House. She kept her head above water as she learned the ropes and was made a director within a year. And, as ever, pushing herself to the limits in the outdoors provided an antidote to the pressure. As well as Munro-climbing, racing sailing on a 33-foot Sigma yacht was her release.

> The racing sailing was important to me. It was great fun. Most of the team worked at BP and, somehow or other, they kept me on an even keel because they understood the industry. I couldn't talk to anyone else about my work because none of my friends understood or had a clue about what I did. So I just didn't tell anyone what I was doing. But it was a massive job.

After five and a half years at Trafalgar House, Vicky moved to North of Scotland Water Authority. So, on that rainy day in September 1996, at the top of Slioch, she was at the end of one era and the beginning of another. Climbing your last Munro has a bit of a tradition about it. The idea is to pick a fairly easy one so that you can invite friends to come along and share in the moment. Slioch is really more of a hard slog than a relaxing hill walk and that combined with the terrible weather made it a less than ideal choice for a final Munro outing.

Still, it was fun. Vicky had invited lots of friends, some ex-colleagues from Trafalgar House, neighbours from Aviemore and her mother. Not everyone was expected to climb so her mother stayed behind at Loch Maree and painted all after-noon and in the evening the company stayed overnight at the local hotel and had a celebratory meal. It was wonderful having so many friends around her that day but there was, too, a slight shadow of anticlimax for Vicky about the climb itself. It was a mixed group of people, all of different ages, backgrounds and levels of fitness and she was concerned that everyone would enjoy the day and not find it too strenuous. In the event, one or two people turned back, the weather was damp, grey and cold, there was no view from the top and, in the end, it all felt a bit flat.

Vicky was thinking, too, with some trepidation, about the meal which was to come that evening because, however much she loves a good meal with good friends, she really does not like being the centre of attention. Everyone was there for her, for her big day, and that was both a joy and a tension. However, it did turn out to be a great evening but, the next day, that little niggle of anxiety began to turn in her mind, that feeling of 'What next?' One might think that a brand-new and very demanding job would be challenging enough and would bring a sense of purpose but not for Vicky.

I was still looking for the thing outside work. Having the chal-lenge of work was great but, on the other hand, what's the other challenge to counter that one? All of a sudden, after I'd completed the Munros, I had a void on one side of my life and I actually felt off-balance. Of course, I continued to go up hills but it wasn't the same. What I ended up doing for a while was taking other people up the hills they wanted to climb and that gave me a bit of satisfaction, for them. But my view had changed because it wasn't a personal and specific challenge I had set myself and, if I didn't get to the top of the hill, I was much less bothered than before. I might pack up early if the weather was bad. And I don't like that way of being at all. I much prefer a sharp focus and a 'let's do it' attitude. I'm not a wanderer. I need a purpose and a goal.

So where was this new thing outside work to come from? Vicky had no idea until, one night in a pub with friends, the conversation drifted to hills and someone asked her what she was going to do now that she had completed the Munros. When she said she didn't know, someone else piped up and suggested, 'Why don't you climb the highest mountain in Europe?' And there it was – the purpose.

As they discussed how to go about finding a guide for Mount Blanc, the idea began to take shape and she decided, 'Yes, I *will* climb Mont Blanc.' Well, no, actually, not Mont Blanc.

Some time later she was busy looking through climbing magazines for a guide to take her up that hill, when she discovered that the highest mountain in Europe is, in fact, not in the Alps but somewhere else entirely. Mont Blanc, on the border of France and Italy, is, at 15,774 feet (4,808 metres), only the highest European mountain west of the Caucasus. It is Mount Elbrus, lying just north of the main Caucasus Range in Russia, which claims the title of the highest peak in the whole of the European land mass; it stands at 18,510 feet (5,642 metres). Now Vicky knew the hill she was aiming for but she had no idea how she was going to get herself to the top.

A few weeks later in March 1997, in her office in Inverness, with the sun streaming through the window, she decided to ring a company she had found in a magazine – OTT Expeditions. The advert said that they did guided trips up Elbrus so, plucking up courage, she dialled the number and spoke to Jon Tinker.

'So, you'd like to go up Elbrus?' he said. 'What have you done up to now?'

Vicky remembers that she stood up for the phone call because it gave her more confidence to be on her feet. Jon's first question made her feel immediately inadequate. 'Well, I haven't done any high altitude, I'm afraid.' She could feel herself shrivelling up with embarrassment.

'Yes but what *have* you done?'

'Well, I've done all of the Munros.'

She heard a splutter at the end of the phone.

'What! Well, you can come!'

Vicky told him she had finished the Munros six months before and he said that was fine but she was still concerned about coming across as more experienced than she felt, so she blurted out, 'But I haven't done any proper climbing!'

'Yes but you'll have done lots of winter climbing on the Munros, won't you?'

'Well, yes', Vicky admitted, 'I've been up in the winter – *walking!* And I've used crampons – *to walk with!* And I've used an ice axe – *walking!* And I've only used ropes once. And I'm not even sure what kit to bring.'

Jon reassured her that technical climbing with ropes would not be required for Elbrus. The mountain can be attempted by any strong hillwalker who knows how to use an ice axe and crampons, which Vicky did. However, it is big and high and, in bad weather, the conditions can become extremely cold and uncomfortable. Jon told Vicky that the trip would include acclimatisation climbs and that OTT would advise on kit and make all the other arrangements. As long as Vicky was fit and strong and had plenty of stamina, she would be fine. And that was it. She was going to climb the highest mountain in Europe – in four months' time.

*   *   *   *   *

'Hello. Are you going to climb Elbrus?'

This was always the difficult part of any trip – meeting a

bunch of complete strangers in the middle of a busy airport. Vicky was feeling rather nervous as she introduced herself to the group at Heathrow and she scanned the faces and physiques surreptitiously for any signs of 'Serious Professional Mountaineer Syndrome'. Would all the others be men who were hugely experienced, enormously fit and very fast? Would they leave her behind on the hill? Her mind had been full of such ridiculous worries in the weeks leading up to Elbrus, weeks spent training on the hills, getting as fit as possible and meticulously organising the kit she was to bring – high altitude boots (plastic ones for warmth, not her faithful leather climbing boots), crampons, fleeces, waterproof trousers, goggles, sunglasses, etc.

The training she had done marked the beginning of a regime which she carefully devised and developed over the years as she prepared herself for the different demands of each of the Seven Summits. Since she had very little idea of what to expect on this trip, she reckoned that she should just try to get as fit as she possibly could. Her training was straightforward – she simply climbed up and down Ben Vorlich as often and as fast as she possibly could. She did other hills as well but she did Ben Vorlich, a Munro on the south side of Loch Earn in Perthshire, repeatedly. It was a handy hill to get to when she was visiting her mother in Balquhidder at weekends. She would climb it several times in the same day, trying to beat her own best time in an effort to get stronger and faster. She did it on her own because, as she remembers with a laugh, 'I was too embarrassed to ask anyone else to do it with me! I mean, it really was daft what I did.'

Normally when she stayed at the cottage she would spend one of the days with her mother and would climb on the other one before driving back up north to Aviemore. As Elbrus loomed larger, however, she would go on the hill on both days of the weekend because she wanted to push her stamina as far as she could. It must have been extraordinarily tedious, slogging up the same hill time after time, day after day. Vicky admits that it was boring but she has an enormous capacity to exclude everything else and focus only on the central goal. Her goal was to become faster and stronger so that was all she concentrated on.

When the time came to pack her kitbag for Elbrus she was as fit and strong as dedication and effort could make her but she still had to face the nightmare of packing everything into one bag. Vicky loathes packing. For days before a trip, her rooms at home are buried under scattered piles of clothing and equipment and scrumpled bits of paper with scribbled lists of things to do and pack. It's torture to sift through them all, packing and re-packing, weighing bits of equipment, selecting one item over another, finding something at the last minute which has to go at the very bottom of the bag, taking everything out and starting all over again. The Elbrus trip was Vicky's first experience of having to pack for a high-altitude climb abroad and for a trip that would last at least two weeks.

> We were only allowed the one kitbag which OTT had sent so there I was, the night before, going through my usual nightmare. I honestly can't remember exactly what I packed or didn't, except that I didn't take a pack of cards and it turned out in the end that we played endless games in the evenings. I made sure that, for future trips, I brought cards. For that first climbing trip abroad, though, as far as I was concerned, I was packing to go into outer space because I had no idea what it would be like. And, in my mind, if I didn't have absolutely everything I required packed into my kit, then that was it – I would fail on the climb.

But it was done at last and, one morning in early July 1997, she was on the plane out of London with the rest of the team. Her fears about finding herself the tyro among a host of experienced high-altitude mountaineers were entirely groundless. As the group began to chat, Vicky realised that everyone was pretty much at the same level. There were about a dozen people on the trip, including three other women and a father and son, and, over the next two weeks, a good camaraderie developed.

The group flew to St Petersburg and spent a couple of days sightseeing and getting to know each other. They took a boat trip to Peter the Great's Summer Palace and also visited the Winter Palace, the sumptuous baroque building on the banks of the River Neva which was, for centuries, the main residence of the Tsars. Today the Winter Palace – and four other buildings ranged along the riverside – house the magnificent Hermitage Museum which boasts one of the world's greatest art collections. The group also met one of their Russian Elbrus guides in St Petersburg who took them to a bar to sample flavoured vodkas. It was all very jolly and relaxing and the point was to try and gel the group before they got down to the real business of climbing mountains.

A train ride to Moscow was followed by a flight south to the town of Mineralnye Vody, the gateway to the Caucasus. The Caucasus range links the Caspian Sea to the Black Sea, forming a natural barrier between the steppes of Russia and the southern states of Azerbaijan, Georgia and Armenia. The main range is a state border between Russia and Georgia but, since it lies just north, Elbrus itself sits inside Russia. By this time, Vicky was getting more and more excited about the prospect of the climb. The conversation and banter with the others were good and they were all enjoying travelling towards their destination. However, after several hours in the back of an old army truck, bumping along on wooden seats and taking turns to change places to avoid the choking black smoke belching from the exhaust pipe, it didn't seem quite so much fun. The further the truck went, the poorer the landscape and towns became – dreary, utilitarian Communist-era apartment blocks covered in graffiti, high-rise buildings standing empty and derelict, except for one light on one landing, featureless scrubland and the occasional drab, sad-looking village market, with the odd mangy dog rummaging about.

Eventually they stopped for the night and, the next day, they set off to climb some training hills for Elbrus. Acclimatisation is a crucial part of any high-mountain climbing. At 18,510 feet Elbrus is one of the lowest of the Seven Summits but, once you get above 10,000 feet, you begin to experience the effects of altitude. There is less oxygen so the effort required to climb is greater. Mount Everest is at the extreme end of the scale but, for Vicky and most of the others on the trip, anything above 4,000 feet was new and alien territory. So the next few days were spent climbing high hills off the Baksan valley, near the border with Georgia. In fact, they were so near the border that, on the first day trekking through the woods by a river, they were startled by two soldiers who jumped out of the bushes and held them up at gunpoint. They turned out to be Russians on patrol. Once the situation was explained, they quickly waved the group on and disappeared again. Later that night, they stayed in a mountain hut and the next day practised on a glacier, climbing up and down, using crampons and ice axes. Vicky was enjoying herself.

The next day, we climbed to the top – quite a hefty climb, amongst boulders and the odd patch of snow. We came down from the top, spent another night in the hut where I helped one of our team, Kath, with her blisters which were starting to get bad. We then drove out to another hill and, this time, we camped. It was another hard slog to the top, back to the tents for a night and that was us ready and acclimatised for Elbrus. It was well organised and good preparation for the real thing.

Mount Elbrus dominates the landscape of the central Caucasus. With its two icy peaks, it rears up like a huge horned creature from the deep valleys and rumpled hills around it. Its two peaks are volcanic vents – the higher western peak, Zapadnaya, being the one Vicky's team would climb. The eastern peak, Vostochnaya, still has a huge crater some 800 feet in diameter. Vostochnaya was first climbed in 1829 and Zapadnaya some forty-five years later in 1874. In more recent times, the mountain was off limits to most climbers until perestroika in the mid 1980s opened up the former USSR. All year round, the mountain top is covered by glacial ice which is hundreds of feet deep in some places.

Vicky cannot now – after more than ten years – remember the name of the village they stayed in at the foot of Elbrus but she remembers the hotel, decorated from floor to ceiling with plastic flowers, red-and-gold painted dolls, coloured plates and brightly painted blinds. She also remembers the surprise of the bus ride up a steep winding road in this old village, past bent peasant women and dilapidated houses, which ended quite suddenly at a massive cable-car station. So Vicky's first steps on her first summit of the seven were on to a cable car rather than the mountain. The cable car took them all the way up to about 15,000 feet, more or less at the snow line, and, from here, the group walked the short distance to the Priutt Hut, an extraordinary four-storey metal-and-wood mountain hut which was sometimes called the highest 'hotel' in the world. It was built in the 1930s and served climbers and skiers for many years until August 1998, the year after Vicky was there, when a group of climbers cooking a meal had an accident with the stove and caused a fire which burned the hut down. In 2001, work began on a ruined fuel storage hut just below the old site and it was cleaned, re-roofed and converted into a new hut with bunk-bedded rooms for about sixty people. Appropriately enough, it is known as the Diesel Hut.

Vicky began to feel the altitude at the Priutt Hut, as did

everyone. It came in the form of headaches and breathlessness. For somebody as fit as Vicky, it was a novel and unpleasant sensation to find herself panting on the way up the stairs.

> The hut was built into the side of a steep slope and outside at the bottom were two loos – 'thunder boxes', as we called them. There were basically two big holes in a wooden platform and, when you looked down into the hole, there was a long drop to a mountain of muck underneath. But the flooring around the holes was rather worn and creaky and rotten so I never felt very safe going to the loo. And it was such an effort. You had to walk all the way down from our third floor by way of a steep wooden staircase and, by the time you got back up to your room, you were panting for breath, chest heaving. It was a bit alarming. I felt so unfit.

They sat for a couple of days at the hut because coming up by cable car to this altitude had been a speedy ascent and they needed to acclimatise. The weather was also poor so they spent their time talking, relaxing and playing cards. Vicky's headaches would come and go but were worst at night, possibly due to the lack of movement and slowing down of the blood flow. At altitude, the blood thickens and you need to drink more water and Vicky had to make a real effort because normally she dislikes drinking a lot of fluids. There was a standpipe outside the top floor but it froze as evening came on so it was important to get as much water inside you during the day in order to avoid having to melt masses of snow in the evening. The more you drink, the more you have to go to the toilet, so there were many exhausting trips to the thunder boxes and back but, in the middle of night, you use your pee bottle. Vicky uses an ordinary water bottle with a screw top, about two-and-a-half inches in diameter. The important thing to remember, of course, is to stick a brightly coloured piece of tape around it, or you may run the risk of drinking from the wrong bottle . . .

The first day of climbing was up through the snow about 1,000 feet to the Pastukhova Rocks and back again. The weather had improved and, on the way back, everyone played around in the snow, sliding on their bottoms, building snowmen and having fun. At altitude, the rule of thumb is climb high, sleep low.

Summit day began in the dark, at about 3 a.m. So far, the climbing had hardly been arduous but this day would be much more demanding. An ascent of 3,000 feet at this altitude is a hard slog but Jon Tinker was very good to his team. As they trooped out of the hut, their head torches bobbing and flickering in the cold darkness, a huge machine suddenly loomed into view. It was a piste-basher, the big machine that smoothes out the snow for skiing, and Jon had arranged for it to drive the team a few hundred feet up towards the Pastukhova Rocks.

After that, it was down to real work. They put on crampons and tramped through crisp snow up to the Rocks, in two groups. The slope was quite steep so they were on what is called walking ropes. Without the ropes, if someone slipped, he or she would travel a very long way. And so they continued for several hours. 'A steady slog' is how Vicky remembers it. They stopped for a quick bite at the col between the two peaks before moving left and up to the western summit. Vicky was in the second group, near the summit, as the first group passed on their way down.

We congratulated them and slapped them on the back as they passed us. They'd left a little can of something alcoholic at the top – gin and tonic, I think it was. So we had our wee celebration at the summit and I remember taking a sip although, with my headache, alcohol was the last thing I wanted! But it was a great feeling to be at the top. And on the way down, as we played about on the glacier, I felt light and happy. 'I've done it! I've been to the top!'

Later that night, though, the excitement of summiting was spectacularly squashed by the nightmare of sickness and diarrhoea at 15,000 feet in a pitch-dark mountain hut, in freezing weather, with no way of getting to a loo. Although she can laugh about it now, Vicky still shudders at the memory of one of the longest nights of her life. When they got down from the summit to the Priutt Hut, there was a big meal of pasta and tomato sauce waiting for them. Vicky is, in her words, 'not very good with tinned tomatoes' because they are quite acidic and, sure enough, in the wee small hours, she became violently ill – from both ends. In the corridor just outside her bunk room was a door leading directly outside to the hill. Vicky knew that she had absolutely no chance of getting down the steep staircase to the thunder boxes as there was no time and it was freezing cold and dark so she did the only thing she could – she staggered to the door at the back, stuck her head outside, threw up into the snow and let everything at the other end run straight into her trousers.

It was just awful! Imagine how cold it was, to be lying there at the door for hours and hours that night. I had to stay there and wait for the next wave and then the next and the next. At one point, I more or less crawled back into the bunk room, scrabbling around in the dark, feeling my way through mounds of clothing and boots and plastic bags for my head torch, some wet wipes and my one spare pair of trousers, desperately hoping no one would wake up and see me. I made it back to the door and cleaned myself up as best I could. It was horrible. And the next day we had to go all the way back down the mountain.

Ah, the joys of mountaineering! Physical discomfort is as much a reality of high-mountain climbing as is the exhilaration of being free as a bird and at one with the glorious natural world. If you cannot stand being cramped in a messy tent with a smelly climber or two, everyone peeing into bottles in the middle of the night; if you cannot cope with the pain of blisters and altitude sickness, and being cold and tired; if you cannot shrug off the thousand little physical aches and niggles that are part and parcel of the game, then it's probably better to read about it, than to do it. Vicky is not interested in reading about climbing, though – she wants to be there, to get to the top and to experience the joys and hardships of being in high places. That night on Elbrus was a bad one but the next day came and she quietly stuffed her ruined clothes into plastic bags at the bottom of her kit and set off with the others, hoping no one would get a whiff of her rucksack on the way down. Actually, although no one had any idea of what had happened, she did tell one of the other climbers the next evening when they were in their hotel. They were sharing a room and he, too, had a dicky tummy and was making such a song and dance about it that she eventually told him about her nightmare experience. At least he had a proper bathroom!

By the time they were safely down and celebrating having climbed Elbrus, Vicky had decided something momentous – she was going to climb the Seven Summits. On the way down from the summit, while they were playing in the snow, someone asked her if she was 'doing the Seven Summits'. She had no idea what they were but, once she knew they included Everest, she made up her mind that this was her new purpose in life – here was a seemingly impossible long-term challenge which would bring balance back into her life and fill the void left by her completion of the Munros.

That night, as the group went out to celebrate, she was enormously excited and energised. Their guides took them to a place in the village which was more like a community centre than a pub. It was huge, smoky and furnished with only a few chairs and tables around an empty central space. A few dog-eared posters hung on the walls. Nobody looked up as the group of western climbers trooped in. Vicky and some others went up to the bar and ordered twelve vodkas to celebrate. What they got was twelve *bottles* of vodka, big milk-bottle-sized vodkas, with no glasses and no water. All that saved Vicky from a massive hangover was the fact that she was still frail from her sickness and could hardly manage to drink anything. The others made up for it, though.

All the way back to Moscow, Vicky was planning her next trip. Elbrus had been much less demanding than she had feared. The headaches from the altitude had been unpleasant but bearable and, although the final push from the col to the summit had been hard, mostly because of the altitude, it had not been seriously difficult. She now had more confidence because she had been higher than ever before and, just as importantly, it had been fun. She had enjoyed being with a group of people, enjoyed the camaraderie and the sightseeing and the shared experience of climbing.

They all went to a nightclub on their last night in Moscow, and it still makes her laugh to remember how they trooped in, wearing shorts, sandals and T-shirts – your basic off-hill kit – and danced the night away in a tiny room surrounded by mirrors. The Russian men spent their time practising their dance moves in front of the mirrors, ignoring the gorgeous women in full make-up, slinky dresses and glittering high heels. It was all rather surreal.

On the way back to London on the plane, Vicky made her plan. Kilimanjaro in Africa would be the next climb – and soon. Through talking to people in the team, she had found out that Kilimanjaro was considered easier than Elbrus – it was higher but in a warmer climate and there were many tracks going to the top. It seemed like the next logical step. She just wanted to get there as soon as she could.

4

UNDER AFRICAN SKIES
KILIMANJARO

It was barely two months before Vicky was packing again. Normally she would never have considered taking more holidays from work so soon – two weeks a year was usually her maximum – but the prospect of tackling her second big summit was so exciting that she could not wait. All her thoughts were directed towards Africa and Kilimanjaro.

The Elbrus climb had given Vicky a lot of confidence. She had been higher than she had ever been before, and had coped well with the altitude and the conditions. She had been confident and happy on the hill, despite the physical rigours and discomforts; even the horrible night of sickness had not put her off wanting to climb higher and harder.

By the time she had arranged her Kilimanjaro trip with a company in the Lake District called KE Adventure, her plan for the rest of the Seven Summits was formed. There are two slightly differing Seven Summit lists, one named after Dick Bass, an American businessman and amateur climber, and the other after the legendary mountaineer Reinhold Messner, who made history with Peter Habbeler in 1980 when they climbed Mount Everest together without supplementary oxygen. Bass's list identified Australia as one of the seven continents, and he therefore climbed the 7,310-foot Mount Kosciuszko in New South Wales, which qualified as the highest peak. He completed his seven by summiting Everest on 30 April 1985 and promptly co-authored a book about it. But Messner thought that as a *mountaineering* continent Australia was hardly significant enough, and he revised the list by including the whole of Australasia. On that basis, the 16,000-foot peak of Carstensz Pyramid (or Puncak Jaya) in Indonesia represented the highest point on the seventh continent. The Canadian mountaineer Pat Morrow completed the peaks on Messner's list in August 1986, and Messner himself shortly afterwards. At the time of writing, more than 100 people have successfully completed the Messner Seven, and more than 150 the Bass list, but it is difficult to be accurate as the websites which gather information are not always up to date.

As she prepared for Kilimanjaro, Vicky had already decided that she would follow the Messner list:

Mount Everest (29,028 ft/ 8,848 m) in Nepal, Asia
Aconcagua (22,834 ft/ 6,960 m) in Argentina, South
　　America
Mount McKinley (20,320 ft/ 6,194 m) (also known as Denali)
　　in Alaska, North America
Kilimanjaro (19,340 ft/ 5,895 m) in Tanzania, Africa
Mount Elbrus (18,510 ft/ 5,642 m) in Russia, Europe
Vinson Massif (16,067 ft/ 4,897 m) in Antarctica
Carstensz Pyramid (16,024 ft/ 4,884 m) (also known as
　　Puncak Jaya) in Papua (formerly Irian Jaya) in Indonesia.

Vicky does not like to read too much about a hill before she tackles it, in case she is put off by detailed descriptions of how difficult or dangerous it is. She reckons that it is better to concentrate on positive preparation and planning, to be clear and serious about the challenge, but not to get bogged down early on in every potential obstacle and difficulty. She does enough research, and talks to enough people, to be meticulous in her planning and rigorous in her training. Very early on she decided the order in which she would climb the Seven Summits, and that she would base her strategy on altitude first, cold second, and then a combination of the two; and she would build up her strength and technical climbing skills towards what seemed to her the most demanding of all: Everest. So, Kilimanjaro would follow Elbrus. The third one, she considered, would need to be higher but still with as little technical difficulty as possible, so she planned to go to the 23,000-foot Aconcagua in Argentina. After that, she calculated, she would need to get experience of a cold environment, but without the altitude. So, having done 23-, 20- and 18-thousand feet, she would go to Antarctica where it is freezing cold, but where the height of the Vinson Massif is only 16,000 feet. At that stage she knew she would be building herself towards one of the hardest climbs – Mount McKinley in Alaska which is cold *and* high (over 20,000 feet); Vicky had been told that if you go to either extremity of the Earth there is less oxygen at altitude, compared with being on the equator. So she knew that 20,000 feet on the equator at Kilimanjaro, and 20,000 feet on Mount McKinley are entirely different. Carstensz Pyramid is neither particularly high nor cold, but it is a technically demanding climb and Vicky planned to do that one as late as possible. And she always knew she would face Everest last; that would be the big one.

For now, though, the immediate challenge was Kilimanjaro, the dormant volcano just inside the Tanzanian border with Kenya in East Africa. Lying 250 miles south of the equator, it is a massive creation, towering above the surrounding arid plains, topped by the glistening white snowy glaciers. Actually, the glaciers have been receding rapidly in recent years and there are fears that the ice which has covered the mountain for nearly 12,000 years may be gone in another twenty. The mountain has two peaks – the volcanic cone, known as Kibo, with its summit crater which is 1.5 miles in diameter, and to the east, Mawenzi. The ascent of Kilimanjaro is a progression through changing natural environments – from the scrubland of the

Masai plains, through the coffee- and plantain-growing areas of its lower southern slopes where the local Chagga people live and work, to lush forests and flowering alpine tundra. The higher one goes, the less vegetation there is, until ice and rock dominate above 15,000 feet.

Vicky made the trip to Kenya in August 1997. With so little time between her return from Elbrus and departure for Kilimanjaro, she had simply continued with her basic training: climbing up and down Ben Vorlich as fast and as often as possible. 'I know every rock of that hill!' she laughs. But she also rang the changes with walking on Cairngorm. At this time she was living in Aviemore and sometimes after work she would drive to the ski lift, park the car and strike off up the hill.

> I used to go straight up over a shoulder, avoiding any paths, and go as hard as I could to the top. I remember reaching the summit in the summer sunset. There was the most beautiful red glow suffusing the clouds, and long shadows lay around me. The heat of the day was receding, and everything was falling quiet. It was lovely, so lovely. I could see for miles and miles, and I remember standing on the top and thinking, 'I'm so lucky to be doing this after work, standing here in the midst of this natural beauty. There can't be many people in a position to do that.' These were stolen moments at the end of my working day, and they were magical.

She felt very fit and strong for Kilimanjaro, although she had no illusions that it would be an easy trip. Kili is not a difficult ascent; it is an extremely popular tourist destination and there are multiple tracks which swarm up the mountain from all sides, including the so-called Coca-Cola Route which draws thousands of hikers and walkers each year because it is the fastest and most direct. There is a more technical climb on the western side which includes the Breach Wall, and the lower peak of Mawenzi is jagged and difficult; only experienced climbers attempt to scale it. (The Western Breach route was closed in January 2006 because of a rockslide.) Still it takes several days to climb to the top of Kilimanjaro and the principal challenge is that, whichever route you take, there is height gain of some 13,000 feet. The altitude is a significant factor.

Vicky had chosen a twelve-day expedition which included acclimatisation trekking on Mount Kenya, the highest mountain in Kenya and the second highest in Africa. She flew into Nairobi and met some of the group at the airport. It was quite a large group, about a dozen people, of mixed ability and background, rather like on Elbrus. They included a few couples, their English guide Chris, and two other women on their own, one Danish and one English. The great character of the group was their local guide for Mount Kenya, Sammy.

> He was a tremendous, larger-than-life character, positive and full of energy. Apart from being an extremely good climber, his claim to fame was that he was a former Kenyan disco-dancing champion! He listened to music all the time while he was climbing and if you were behind him you would see him dancing and doing all the moves as he climbed. I remember at one point on the hill I was ahead of the rest and Sammy and I were waiting. He lay down on his back and started disco-dancing as he listened to his Walkman; then he handed one of the earphones to me and the two of us lay there, on the slopes of Mount Kenya, dancing on our backs.

Mount Kenya has three summits. Two of them, Batian and Nelion, require technical climbing on ice or rock. Point Lenana, the third peak, rises to about 16,000 feet and it took two or three days of hiking to reach it. Vicky suffered from altitude headaches a little at the top hut where they overnighted before the scramble to the summit. Otherwise it was a pleasant and relaxing few days. The mountain sits in Mount Kenya National Park which is home to a huge variety of flora and fauna, including cape buffalo, eland, zebra and the hyrax, or 'rock rabbit', a cat-sized mammal with a grey/brown coat which looks a bit like a very large shrew. They were scrabbling about all over the place among the vegetation on the way down the hill. Vicky liked them, but didn't care much for the monkeys which were everywhere at the big campsite at the foot of the mountain.

They would come and pinch your food and you had to be careful that they didn't scratch you as they grabbed for it. We had two tents between three girls, and it was my turn to be in a tent on my own. I didn't like it at all. I kept thinking the monkeys would get in during the night, and when I had to get up to go to the loo I had to walk across the open ground, in the dark, past a building and on to the loo hut. And these monkeys were everywhere! Hundreds of them swinging from the trees, sitting on the roofs, watching you and jumping down. I kept expecting one to land on my head while I was squatting!

They returned to Nairobi and from there it was a bus-ride across the border into Tanzania. Their destination was Kilimanjaro National Park and, as they were getting nearer, Vicky vividly remembers the driver suddenly stopping the bus at the side of the road and calling over his shoulder:

'You can all get out now and have a look.'
   This was a two-lane, quite busy road. We got out of the bus, but we didn't know what we were supposed to be looking at.
   'You want to see Kilimanjaro?'
   'But where is it?'

'Look up!'

So we looked up – and up, and up. And then we saw it. We had been looking out at the low hills on the horizon, and the clouds above them – but we hadn't looked above the clouds. And there it was, peeking out from the top of the clouds, just the topmost tip of Kilimanjaro. But because we were actually quite close, it looked enormous! And we all thought, 'Are we expected to get all the way up there?'

Of all the hills I climbed, I never had that kind of view, even with Everest. It looked absolutely mammoth and we looked at each other in consternation. I remember that up to that moment I'd been thinking, 'Hey ho, this is going to be fine', and then suddenly – this!

That night Vicky was again on her own, in a horrible, grimy room in the hotel in Arusha village. Actually, not entirely on her own since there was an enormous cockroach that scuttled around all night. She cannot bear cockroaches and lay, either watching it or listening to it, throughout the night. She would have swapped the cockroach for a manic monkey any day . . .

The next morning they hopped on the bus again, drove to the park, signed in at the wee registration hut and started to walk. Their route was Machame, one of the less busy ones (at least in 1997), which involves a six-day hike to the summit. The track began by following steep paths through the rainforest, and the group trekked through dense vegetation and huge amounts of mud. It was misty and humid among the big-leaved trees which dripped with great swathes of moss. They continued upwards by short sections of steep climbs until they emerged through the forest and reached their first campsite. Every group on Kilimanjaro must use porters and local guides, so at the end of each day the tents would be erected and food cooked. The campsite was not very pleasant; it was rather dirty and insanitary. Compared with Everest Base Camp, Vicky remembers, it was absolutely filthy. The next day they continued to climb through increasingly sparse trees and bushes until they reached moorland. They camped that night on a small plateau from where they could look north-west towards the Kibo summit, and eastwards to Mount Meru.

It was not a hard climb, but it demanded stamina and strength. Once they reached the high Barafu camp, at about 17,000 feet, ready for summit day, the mountain landscape had changed utterly. They were well above the tree line, and all around were rocks, scree and bare mountain, and high on the summit the crown of snow and ice. It was a very early start for the summit: they got up at midnight and set off about one in the morning. The ascent usually takes between five and seven hours and the idea is to get as high as possible before the sun rises and the heat of the day descends. Vicky had been coping extremely well with the altitude, but as dawn approached and she pushed up the long steep climb to Stella Point, from the rim of the Kibo crater, she began to feel utterly exhausted.

When we reached the summit lip, we turned left and the trail continues around the edge of the crater another few hundred feet up to the summit. But when I got to the lip I thought, 'I can't go any further. There's no way I'm going to manage the rest.' I had absolutely no energy. But then everyone else set off, leaving me at the back, and I said to myself, 'Don't be ridiculous. Just get on with it.' It wasn't a steep climb, just a series of what I call 'little uppy bits', but they were huge obstacles for me. But I dug in and got on with it.

In the end, it had been a slog, but she got there and on the summit, with Mount Meru in the distance, peeping above the clouds, there were smiles and congratulations. One of the team, a Welshman, had brought a Welsh flag wrapped around his ice axe, so he unfurled it at the top in celebration. For Vicky it was very much a communal celebration; they had climbed as a group and although she was thrilled to have reached her second big summit, this was not such an intensely personal achievement as some of the later ones, like Mount McKinley and Vinson Massif and, of course, Everest, where she had to draw on her deepest and toughest reserves of physical and mental strength.

But Kilimanjaro had still made demands. And on the way down there was a stark reminder that, no matter how popular the mountain is and no matter how many thousands of people climb it every year, it is still very high: as they descended, they came across a woman who was suffering from serious altitude problems. Her lungs were rumbling, which means that they were beginning to fill with fluid. Chris, the guide and ex-nurse, looked at her and advised her to go down immediately. For one woman at least, the trek to the top of Kilimanjaro was beyond reach.

5

HIGH IN THE ANDES
ACONCAGUA

Some of the best times Vicky had when she returned from climbing were when she visited her mother to tell her all about the trips. They would put on a pot of coffee, settle themselves in the living room, Maureen would light up a cigarette and spread the photographs all over the table, and Vicky would talk her mother through the climb, the other people in the group, the weather, the landscape, and all the funny things that happened. Her mother was interested in everything. She was a really good listener and although, by unspoken consent, Vicky did not describe – and her mother did not ask about – the parts of a climb that may have been dangerous, or the times where Vicky had felt ill or exhausted, still these 'downloads', as Vicky calls them, were very precious to her. Most people she worked with, apart from her closest colleagues, did not know that she climbed hills, or that she was tackling the Seven Summits; her hillwalking friends knew, but Vicky didn't want to press them with too many of what were, essentially, her holiday snaps. So it was her mother with whom she could most enthusiastically share her tremendous excitement at having been to Elbrus and Kilimanjaro, her mother who would never tire of hearing all about her adventures and plans for the next climb.

The next climb after Kilimanjaro was, Vicky knew, going to be a big one. Aconcagua, in the Argentine Andes near the border with Chile, is the highest mountain in South America;

in fact, at 22,834 feet (6,960 metres) it is the highest point in the Western and Southern hemisphere, and the second highest of the Seven Summits. This is the mountain which all the guidebooks describe as technically easy (if you climb by the normal route which Vicky did), but never to be underestimated: its height can be deadly, because it can cause severe altitude sickness and because of the extreme cold and devastating winds which can occur above 16,400 feet. In his book, *Seven Summits – The Quest to Reach the Highest Point on Every Continent,* the British mountaineer Steve Bell writes that about 3,000 climbers a year attempt the summit of Aconcagua, by various routes; with a success rate of less than 50 per cent, this is not a hill to be trifled with. (I am indebted to this book, published in 2000 under the general editorship of Steve Bell, for many interesting facts about, and descriptions of, the Seven Summits.)

Vicky was still on a tremendous high when she got back to Scotland from Kilimanjaro. As ever, she started planning right away, although it would be nearly a year before she would be ready to tackle Aconcagua. The best months for climbing the mountain are December to March, so she once again contacted OTT Expeditions, with whom she had climbed Elbrus, and arranged to go in December 1998. She wanted to book the trip as quickly as possible, while she was still energised.

When the blood's up, you want to do it. And I knew that the longer I left it, the more time I would have to think, 'Hang on, what am I doing?' But if you're committed to a plan and a date, you'll do it.

She also knew that the trip would last at least three weeks from beginning to end, and she had to fit it in with her job at North of Scotland Water. She was under extreme time pressures to introduce the new working conditions and job evaluations so, once again, she planned her life around the day job and the hill training.

This time, however, she knew it would not be enough simply to run up and down Ben Vorlich two or three times a day. Aconcagua was new territory, higher than she had ever been before, and there would be no porters on the long, steep ascent after Base Camp, so she would be carrying a heavier pack than ever before. She joined a gym in Inverness and went after work, three times a week if she could manage. She hated every minute of it but persevered because she knew that the sessions on the bicycle and the step machine, the endless lifting and pushing of weights and the floor exercises would pay off in the end. And there was also the little flicker of satisfaction at lifting heavier weights than some of the men in the gym . . .

I was pushing very heavy weights on a special machine for your legs, and these guys would stroll up to the machine as soon as I'd finished, and bend down nonchalantly to adjust the weight upwards – and their jaws would drop when they saw what I'd been doing. I loved that!

It was while she was preparing for Aconcagua that Vicky also introduced her trademark training tool – the telephone directories. Practically every article which has been written about her describes how 'this slight, wiry woman trained for Mount Everest by climbing Munros with telephone directories in her backpack'. It is such a delightfully eccentric, home-made image which somehow makes it easier to identify with her achievement as being that of an ordinary person, rather than an elite mountaineer. She always laughs herself about the quirkiness of stuffing a backpack with up to sixteen telephone directories and then pushing herself up hills, but as a training technique it certainly paid off. She knew that she would be carrying a tent, sleeping bag, mat, thin inflatable thermarest mattress and kit up Aconcagua and that her pack would be much bigger than the thirty-five-litre daypacks she had carried up the Munros and Elbrus. On Kilimanjaro there had been porters. So she bought a bigger pack, filled it with directories, and every weekend found her on the hills, come rain or shine. All her hillwalking friends knew about the directories, and there are plenty of stories about being on the hills with Vicky and her phone books. Ron Swanson, a friend from Forres, recalled how his son, Jamie, was coming down off a hill after a very long day's climbing with Vicky. They decided to phone ahead to the nearest pub to book dinner because they knew they would arrive very late. They had a mobile phone, but no number for the pub so, exhausted, they sat down in the gloaming by the edge of the track while Vicky laboriously unpacked her sixteen phone books to find the correct one for the area. She had practically every directory for Scotland – except the one they were looking for, of course. It never occurred to either of them to phone directory enquiries.

About a week before she set off for Aconcagua, when her training was at its most intensive, Vicky decided to dash up a hill outside Aviemore one Saturday morning, before she set off down the road to visit her mother in Balquhidder. She loaded up her rucksack with the phone books and set off up the hill. It got colder and colder, and windier and windier; then it started to snow and quite suddenly she was engulfed in a whiteout.

There's a track up one side and down the other, but I couldn't see it for the snow. I wasn't nervous because I knew the hill well and I could have come back down. I just needed to concentrate. But it was still pretty foul weather, and there I was on the hill in the middle of it. And I remember sitting down and starting to giggle. I had no telephone with me but I had all these telephone directories in my pack and I had a sudden vision of the newspaper headline the next day – 'Lone woman climber found frozen to death on hill, weighed down by phone directories.' It was just so silly!

However, nothing worse happened to her that day than being stopped by the police for speeding down the A9 on the way to her mother's. They were curious about the three weeks' worth of shopping in the back of car which she had bought to keep her mother stocked up while she was away climbing; and they were also intrigued by the fact she was going to Argentina to climb a mountain. 'Aye, well – John would have been very interested in that if he'd been here,' they told her. 'He's a climber himself.' Unfortunately, John wasn't on duty that day and they fined her anyway. She didn't care: the following week she was off to South America, leaving speeding tickets and telephone directories behind.

*   *   *   *   *

Mendoza, 11 December 1998
Hot, sunny and humid. Hotel has a small but nice swimming pool. I shared a room with Shirley from Brentwood. People in this large group seem to be fine.

Vicky's diary entries tend to be short and to the point, scribbled on scraps of paper rather than in notebooks, and Everest is the only one of the Seven Summits where she kept a substantial journal, partly because it was the longest and most demanding trip and partly because there was so much time at Base Camp to sit and write. For Aconcagua, however, all she brought back by way of a journal was a couple of crumpled A4 lined pages, written on both sides and folded into four. The entries stop after she reaches Base Camp. When you have to carry every single item on your back, thousands of feet up a mountain, you tend to want to reduce the weight in any way possible. It weighs less to have a few scraps of paper than a bound notebook. And this extends to every item of kit. Vicky carries a pencil instead of a biro because the pump in a biro will not work well at altitude, and the ink will freeze. Around the end of the pencil she winds the strong, sticky gaffer tape which every climber needs for things like running repairs on ripped trousers and mending goggles. It saves space and weight to carry the tape this way, rather than taking a big heavy roll with a hole in the middle. Vicky learnt many tricks like that over the years on the hills and they became invaluable for keeping the pack weight down on Aconcagua.

It's all about weight and space in your pack. Take packaging off things, and put things like vitamin pills in a plastic bag, with the exact number you need counted out. Don't take a pot of cream because that will be heavy. Squirt it into a plastic bottle instead. Some people even cut the handle off their toothbrush to save weight and space. They are absolutely paranoid about weight, and some won't even take toothpaste. I take a tiny little tube and ration it. And loo rolls: I take one roll, unwind it from the cardboard tube, throw that away and just take the paper.

There was plenty of time to pack and unpack, re-arrange items and check everything at Aconcagua Base Camp. The acclimatisation which had started several days before would continue here until the group was ready to climb higher. It had been a long journey in from Mendoza, in western Argentina. The city stands on the main road between Argentina and Chile and the surrounding area is the heart of the country's wine-producing region. Vicky had met most of the Aconcagua group at São Paolo airport in Brazil, but it was only once they were settled into their hotel in Mendoza that the process of getting to know each other began. It was a large, diverse group of thirteen climbers, plus the guide, Andy Broom, and his partner. There was a retired train-driver, a policeman from Newcastle and a man whom everyone called 'Falkland John' because he was in charge of maintenance for the British Army garrison in the Falkland Islands. Also in the group was a man who worked as a trainer in a gym and he was making a film of the climb. Vicky's room- and tent-mate was Shirley, a marathon runner from Essex who worked in marketing. She and Vicky were to become good friends over the next few weeks. Then there was 'Dagenham Dave', or 'Daggers', so-called not because he was from Dagenham but because it was a nickname he was given by a friend – 'two stops short of Barking' – which, says Vicky, 'couldn't have been further from the truth'. The fittest members of the team were two young men who were going to climb by a much harder route, the Polish Glacier on the east face, named after a group of Polish climbers who first made this ascent alpine style (that is, without stop-ping at fixed camps) in 1934. The group also included an HR manager, an engineer called Chris Boggon, who was Dagenham Dave's mate and with whom Vicky was later to climb Mount McKinley, and a husband and wife who, Vicky vividly remem-bers, wore matching 'his and hers' climbing kit.

It does depend on your own personality, how much you enjoy this kind of haphazard coming together of strangers; Chris describes the group as 'rather odd, socially, with one or two misfits – apart from myself!' and he spent much of the time with his pal, Daggers, whom he had climbed with in the Himalayas. One gets the distinct impression that he preferred to keep to the outside edges of the strange, assorted group. Vicky, on the other hand, is rather comfortable in this kind of setting, just quietly getting along and making friends, occupying her own space but very happy to join in with everyone else as well. She has a strong sense of team dynamics and the impor-tance of good relationships on the hill. These things do matter at 20,000 feet in the cold and dark when everyone is tired and out of sorts, and you are all trying to get to the top of the highest mountain in the southern hemisphere. As it turned out, several people would not reach the summit.

They left Mendoza by bus and drove for three hours through dusty, barren, rocky countryside that is only occasionally relieved by small farms and cultivated land. Men on horses trotted by. Their destination was Puente del Inca, a small Andean village at nearly 9,000 feet, very near the border with Chile. The name means 'the Inca's Bridge', and refers to the span of rock which forms a natural bridge over the Vacas River. Nearby there are hot springs which stain the rocks a sulphurous yellow and were the reason for the big thermal resort and spa which was built in the early years of last century. Nowadays the area is a popular ski resort. The group spent a night in a hotel, and the next day set off in Land Rovers to Aconcagua National Park. In the distance they caught their first sight of Aconcagua's south face, steep and severe and icy. Vicky's diary entry reads simply, 'Wow – what a hill.' Aconcagua is a big, wedge-shaped mountain. Its name means 'stone sentinel' and although the South Face is an 8,000-foot wall of rock and ice, the mountain rises just east of the main Andean chain, in the smaller Frontal Range, a region which is arid and barren and receives much less snowfall than the main range. Consequently, great areas of Aconcagua are wind-battered bare rock and scree. Even the surrounding valleys lack many trees or much vegetation, except for grasses and bushes. With the sun beating down and the wind blowing great clouds of dust for miles, this is a tough landscape.

Once inside the national park, with the register signed and stamped so that the authorities knew how many people were going on the hill, the walking started. A neat line of mules appeared with local men, and the food and tents and equipment were loaded up for the long trek to Base Camp. They would go on ahead and the group would follow more slowly so that they could fit in some acclimatisation climbs along the way, close to the south face of the mountain. They followed a trail along the Horcones River for about five miles to the confluence of the Lower and the Upper Horcones Rivers. After crossing the Lower Horcones on a footbridge, they continued up the river valley towards Confluencia (over 11,000 feet) where they camped for the night. The next morning they trekked up the valley for three or four hours to the foot of the south face which Vicky's diary described as 'pretty jaggy and vicious and snowy'. At this stage they were high enough — well over 12,000 feet — for the constant incline to cause some breathlessness, but it would help to get them ready for the real thing.

The next day the long trek up through the wide and broad Horcones Valley, all the way around the south side of the mountain, began in earnest.

The valley was extraordinary and spectacular. The rocks were stained and coloured and striated by all the different minerals, and the track went very gently uphill, for miles and miles and miles; you feel as if you're getting nowhere. You try to monitor your progress against the hills on either side, but even that is no good because they're so huge. There were rivers, and rocks and scree gouged out by the slow grinding of the glacier which formed this valley, and the sun was beating down on us.

On and on they trudged, hour after hour through what is basically a massive dry river-bed known as the Playa Ancha, the Long Beach. This river-bed was criss-crossed with numerous other small glacial rivers which were fast and freezing, many of which they had to wade through up to their knees. After the Beach section, the trail began to rise steadily by a series of scrambles and descents on dirt, gravel and rocks. It was hot, sweaty, heart-pumping going. The wind was in their faces, blowing up great swirling mists of rough, grainy sand. Daggers was got up like some cattle-rustling cowboy, with a big scarf tied across his face, and several other people had draped towels over their heads to protect the backs of their necks from the sun. The couple in their matching kits brought up the rear, happy in their own company. During the long day other groups of climbers bound for the mountain passed them, and then late in the afternoon, in a great clatter of hooves and cloud of dust, a group of gaucho horsemen trotted up, driving a herd of mules, whoop-whooping and shouting. Each time a mule made a bid for escape or wandered off in the wrong direction, the gaucho would sit up in his wooden saddle, whirl the three-balled *bolas* above his head and fling it at the legs of the mule to bring it down. As far as Vicky was concerned, this was better than being at the cinema, although she suspected there was a good deal more whoop-whooping and *bolas*-throwing going on than was strictly necessary. The urge to put on a show for the rag-tag bunch of white-limbed, sweating, sun-burned, tea-towel wrapped British tourists must have been too tempting for words.

When they finally reached Base Camp at Plaza de Mulas (14,300 feet) after fourteen miles and eight hours of trekking, the first casualties of the climb occurred. Two members of the team were floored by altitude sickness and had to be taken back down immediately. One of them was Dagenham Dave, who was suffering from sickness, headaches and breathlessness, and before the evening light faded both men left the camp. Dave was in such a bad way that he could barely sit up on the back of the mule; Vicky watched his figure for a long time, slumped forward and swaying, as the woebegone procession wound its way back down the valley. It cast a shadow over the pleasure of reaching Base Camp.

The next morning Vicky, Shirley and Falkland John spent part of the day walking across the valley to an old hotel which was once used by climbers as a Base Camp.

It was rather bizarre to find it here, in the middle of nowhere. It had a bar and we sat drinking fruit juice and watching what was going on. A handful of folk were staying in the hotel, and one or two had pitched tents outside. There were a few guys playing guitars, singing and welcoming us with lazy smiles. It was all very laid-back and relaxed. And we certainly weren't in any hurry. When you're acclimatising like this you've got hours to hang around your tent and fret about your packing, or just wander around. We sat and chatted, then explored the valley a bit further, enjoying our environment and getting used to the altitude. I think that's very important and I find it very comforting, somehow, not to be rushing through a place. I enjoy taking the time.

It was just as well that Vicky and Shirley enjoyed one another's company because when you share a tent with a stranger, you need to be able to get on. They were two very different people, with different personalities, but they hit it off.

Shirley was great fun and she told great jokes. I actually get quite tense when I'm climbing, so she helped me calm down and enjoy myself. When we were in the tent she would get out her cleansing lotion, and she'd be busy applying it with a cotton wool pad. All I had was my one pot of heavy-duty sun cream and that was it. And she had mascara, too. But she didn't appear to be carrying more weight than me. She was very, very efficient. I can't remember whether I even had a hairbrush or not. I saw a picture of myself on the summit, much later, and my hair is absolutely plastered to my head. That's what several weeks of no brushing or washing and sleeping with a hat on will do for you. I looked a sight!

After a couple of days at Base Camp it was time to set off for Camp 1. The route to the summit would be the so-called Normal Route by the north-west ridge. In twos and threes they climbed through more rocky, arid terrain and at one point came across the natural phenomenon of *los penitentes,* tall shards of snow, like stalagmites, which looked as if they were growing out of the rock. These strange formations, frozen and then warmed by the sun, stood like jaggy, white forests. By this stage, everyone was carrying full packs and it was hard going up the rocky slopes where you could easily slip back in the scree. By the time they reached Camp 1 it was starting to snow, and the next morning everything was covered in a thick white blanket.

Camp 2, at 17,500 feet, is well named – Nido del Condores, the condors' nest. It sits on a broad, windy shoulder of the mountain at the top of a punishing steep slope, but with a stunning view up to the vast scree field called Gran Accareo, and rising above it the Canaleta Couloir which leads to the summit. It was at this camp that the group was further reduced. All the way from Base Camp, the fitness trainer had been climbing strongly, pushing ahead and going faster than everyone else, often leaving the group far behind. Suddenly, and for no reason that Vicky or anyone else heard about, he decided at Camp 2 that he was not going any further and he went down again, accompanied by the policeman who was suffering from flu. By this stage, too, Jim the train driver was beginning to suffer from the altitude, but was adamant that he would get to the summit. The weather was bitterly cold and windy and up there life and relationships were just a bit harder. Everyone hunkered down for the night in preparation for the climb to Berlin Camp, the staging post for the summit.

*   *   *   *   *

In the pre-dawn darkness Vicky and Shirley flicked on their head torches and quickly got ready for the climb to the summit. Neither of them said much. When it's bitterly cold and dark, and you're squashed in a tiny tent 19,500 feet up in the Andes, being buffeted by winds, when your head is thumping and your stomach churning, there's not generally much small talk goes on. Here they were at Berlin Camp, perched on a cold and exposed slope of rocks, scree and patches of snow and, rolling into the distance below them, mile upon mile of glorious mountains and ridges. By this time, although she did not know it, Vicky's face was badly swollen from the altitude, and her headaches were becoming worse. Her face felt rather odd, with numb patches around the temples, but she put it down to the general discomfort she was feeling, rather than a specific altitude symptom. Yesterday had been a long day: a steep, demanding trudge from Camp 2, followed by hours of sitting around in tents at Berlin, resting in preparation for summit day. There are several small A-frame, wooden huts at Berlin, in various states of disrepair, not tall enough to stand up in but providing shelter from the driving wind. They used them as their mess tents, and in the wee small hours of summit day the team was now huddled inside together, squatting on wooden planks on the snow, trying to force down some tea and porridge. Chris was suffering badly from headaches and had doubted the day before whether he would be well enough to get to the summit, but now he was ready to go.

This is the stage of a climb where, if you don't climb high mountains, you might wonder where the attraction is when life is this uncomfortable. Is there not a time when Vicky ever just wishes she were in a nice hot bath with a good book, rather than sitting on a cold, dark mountain, feeling sick? Apparently not.

You rise above it because you want to do something badly enough. I never thought, 'I wish I were back home'. But I knew home was always there. I never thought to myself, 'You have to stick this discomfort out because the next hill will be even tougher'. Because, once I'm on a hill, I'm only thinking of that hill. I'm not thinking ahead to the next one. If I'd allowed that to happen, I might have sunk along the way. So it's about very,

very strong focus and mental discipline. And I know people say rather flippantly, 'It's not the physical strength, it's the mental strength', but it's true. And how do you train for mental strength? For me, it's all those years of going out and bashing the hills in Scotland in all weathers. Yes, it develops physical stamina, but it's actually mental stamina that gets you up there. You're pushing yourself through hardships, like the bad weather, the scary bits, the fatigue. And it's fun! In the midst of everything, it's fun and it's exciting and it's where I want to be.

So there she was, on Christmas Day 1998, in the cold and dark, exactly where she wanted to be – on her way to the top of Aconcagua. The group set off, slowly zig-zagging up the north-west ridge on crampons and ice axes. Several hours after the dawn they came upon the ruins of Refugia Independencia, the highest refuge hut in the world at 21,476 feet. They crossed a small col and then the Gran Accareo opened in front of them, a massive, open 35-degree scree slope which climbs all the way to the deep gully of Canaleta. Vicky was finding it hard and she remembers that she was going rather slowly at this stage. Canaleta is the feature people talk about as being the most difficult on the normal Aconcagua route, but it was the slog up Gran Accareo which Vicky found harder. The Canaleta was tough, though. This 30-degree gully rises 1,300 feet to the summit ridge and is basically a chute filled with loose rocks and stones which slither and give way as you climb. Some of the boulders are large and you must rely on the people above you not to dislodge them on to your head. The hours passed and the effort increased. At this altitude every step, every stumble, drains your energy and you need frequent rests, and by the time Vicky hauled herself up the last few feet of the Canaleta she was puffing hard. From there all that remained was the climb along the Cresta del Guanaco, the ridge which links the lower south summit to the higher north one.

At last they were there, 22,834 feet high in the Andes, gazing out over a 360-degree panoply of snow-topped 20,000-foot peaks, some obscured by the clouds, others rising gloriously to the open sky. At the top was a small aluminium cross, fixed into the rock. Everyone congratulated each other and photos were taken. They stood in twos and threes, looking and talking, but not for very long; it's cold and windy on the summit and a long way back down again.

They overnighted at Camp 3 and then descended all the way to Base Camp. It was then that they discovered a present left by Dagenham Dave: his mother had baked him a Christmas cake for the trip and he had generously left it for everyone before he had been transported off the mountain with altitude sickness. There was much merriment and eating in the Mess Tent that night, and many toasts to absent friends. 'Cheers, Daggers!' 'Here's to Daggers' mum! Thanks, Mrs Owen!' When she got back home, Vicky wrote to Mrs Owen to thank her for giving them such a lovely Christmas present to enjoy, high in the mountains of Argentina.

All that remained was the long walk-out again, but for Shirley and Vicky it turned out to be an epic journey. Shirley developed the most appalling blisters on both feet and as the miles and hours wore on, trudging down the rocky valley, wading through rivers, slipping and crunching through thick scree, the pain became severe. Her feet were raw and bleeding. Every time she had to ford a river, she had to take off her boots and put them on again on damp feet, covered in grit and sand. It was a nightmare for her. Everyone else had grad-ually got further ahead, but Vicky didn't want to leave Shirley. As the pain of the blisters worsened, Shirley became more frustrated and angry, shouting at Vicky to leave her alone and go ahead. So eventually Vicky would move ahead a bit, then lurk behind a rock or dip and wait until she was sure Shirley was still on her feet. The sun was beating down, the dust was swirling and the miles were inching past with glacial slowness.

But finally the grassy meadow of the trail head appeared and Vicky's spirits soared. They had done it! Back at the hotel in Puente del Inca, while poor Shirley tended her wounds – to this day Vicky is in awe of the pain barriers she went through on the fourteen-mile walk-out – the others were already celebrating. They had made it. *She* had made it, to the top of the highest mountain she had ever climbed, and back down again. Vicky felt as if she were floating an inch above the ground. It was the best feeling in the world.

6

THE WHITE SOUTH
VINSON MASSIF

The attic is long and low, with one tiny window looking out to the hill behind the house. From one end to the other the space is filled with boxes, neatly taped and stacked, big, rectangular plastic containers, about three or four feet long by two feet deep, a large black plastic dustbin and an even bigger blue plastic barrel. Each box, barrel and container has a sticker on the top or side with the contents neatly printed in black felt-tip pen. There are plastic bags which jingle with metal clips and climbing harnesses. One box contains lethal-looking pairs of crampons; another plastic bag is full of different lengths of rope.

This is the roof space above Vicky's kitchen. This is her equipment room, where the stories of her climbs are told in the neatly rolled-up sleeping bags which have been around the world from Africa to South America, and the unfeasibly huge and heavy pair of boots which lean against a smaller pair patched with tape where crampons have nicked them; in the multiple pairs of bear-sized mittens and thick socks, and the all-in-one down body suits to repel the cold of the Antarctic and the Himalayas; in the stack of rucksacks in the corner, of varying sizes, and the inflatable air mat which is always a pain to deflate and flatten in the morning. Vicky moves around the boxes, pulling out one piece of clothing and equipment after another – 'I sewed this little Union Jack on to this down suit for my first attempt on Everest' – and describing how to attach different things to a harness, how to choose between an all-in-one suit and jacket and trousers, and how to fix on a pair of crampons. Each item has a time and a place and a story attached to it. She picks up a pair of thick gloves, scarred with rope burns from the descent on her first attempt on Everest. 'That was very, very scary, coming down a steep slope, not abseiling but facing down the slope, with the rope wound through my arm and hand. It was horrible.' Standing in this cramped space, surrounded by the physical links to the high places Vicky has climbed, brings the reality a little nearer. The jangle of a harness loaded with karabiners is more vivid than a verbal description, especially when you pick it up and feel the weight. A scarred glove speaks louder than a summit photograph.

The principal reason for climbing up the metal ladder into the attic was to find the big down jacket which Vicky bought for climbing the Vinson Massif in Antarctica, her fourth summit of the seven. She wanted to demonstrate just how enormous it is and, true enough, when she put it on she looked instantly like the Michelin man in the advert. The jacket is a vivid orangey yellow, filled with down and very heavy. After a couple of minutes' modelling it, Vicky was so warm she had to take it off. When she was preparing her kit for Antarctica she visited her mother to tell her all about the trip, and Maureen, with her usual enthusiasm, asked to try on the jacket. Standing in the attic, Vicky remembered the moment:

> At that stage my mother was a very small, slight person and she virtually disappeared when she put it on! She could hardly stand up in the thing! She said, 'Can I go and look in the mirror?' And, when she saw herself, she couldn't believe it. There was pride but, at the same time, she couldn't believe that anyone would need that level of warmth. I had always tried to keep her involved in my trips and tell her what I was doing, trying to keep it light-hearted, assuring her I would be

fine, and at the same time gently letting her know that I was going to an extreme place. We both knew, although we did not discuss it, that Antarctica is an extreme place.

A few weeks later, crawling through a blizzard, battered by 100 m.p.h. winds, Vicky would experience the reality of battling for survival in an extreme place.

*   *   *   *   *

To go to Antarctica is not just to visit another country; it is to travel to another world. By the time Vicky was back at work in January 1999 after her successful summiting of Aconcagua, her mind was full of the thrilling vision of climbing in the icy wilderness of Earth's last frontier continent. She was going to the coldest, windiest, driest place on the planet, a vast land entombed in an ice sheet miles deep, where the lowest recorded temperatures in winter have reached -89°C (-129°F) and tremendous winds, flowing from the South Pole, some 9,000 feet above sea level, gather speed as they descend to the coast and scream across the ice at speeds reaching 185 m.p.h. This was the fierce and magnificent place where Robert Falcon Scott and his party died in a blizzard, exhausted and starving, on their way back from the South Pole in March 1912. A few years later, Sir Ernest Shackleton's 1914–16 expedition to cross the continent ended in near disaster when his ship, *Endeavour*, was crushed in the pack ice. He and his men managed to get to Elephant Island by sledge and boat, from where a small party led by Shackleton made a heroic and perilous voyage of 800 miles to South Georgia where they organised rescue for the men left behind. His story of that epic expedition is called, simply, *South*, and is dedicated to 'my comrades who fell in the white warfare of the South and on the red fields of France and Flanders'. This dangerous and beautiful world has drawn explorers and adventurers into its icy embrace for more than a century. This, perhaps more than any other in her Seven Summits challenge, was the destination which fired Vicky's imagination and set her pulse racing, not because of the mountain she was to climb, but because of where it was, a tiny part of this vast white continent of dreams and nightmares.

She was well aware that, yet again, she was stepping up to a new level. Vinson Massif, on the southern part of the main ridge of the Sentinel Range, is thirteen miles long, eight miles wide and 16,067 feet (4,897 metres) high. By the standards of Aconcagua or Everest, it is neither particularly high nor is it a technical climb, but the environment is hostile and the levels of fitness, stamina and endurance required are considerable. One of the many climbing websites dedicated to Vinson states simply: 'We cannot over-emphasise the importance of physical conditioning.' Vicky booked with a company called Jagged Globe. There was the usual questionnaire about her experience and a couple of phone calls. The many, many companies which offer to guide non-professional climbers up the Seven Summits are businesses whose aim is to make money; the more people they attract, the more money they make. But it is also in their interests to make sure that people get to the top of the hills, so they need to be careful about whom they accept, which is why they ask questions about previous experience. Once they knew that she had been to the top of Elbrus and Aconcagua (Kilimanjaro did not register) and had climbed all the Munros, she was in. Interestingly, the Munros have been Vicky's trump card throughout the Seven Summits. All these years of climbing Scotland's high hills, especially in the winter time, qualified her as a fit, strong, reliable climber for mountains all over the world. In fact, when she was in the Antarctic a young American climber teased her about Scotland's hills when she told him what the Munros were. 'You've climbed hills that are only 3,000 or 4,000 feet, and you're here to climb Vinson! You call that climbing!' The following year, he came to Scotland himself and climbed in the Cairngorms. Vicky received an ecstatic email from him, apologising for his teasing and saying that he had enjoyed the most fantastic climbing and that he would be back the next year.

When Vicky approached Jagged Globe about the possibility of climbing Vinson, they told her they knew of one other person who wanted to go. They organised a guide to take both climbers and the trip was booked for November 1999 (the best time to go to the Antarctic is during the summer months when there is twenty-four-hour daylight). They sent her the kit and equipment list which included a five-season sleeping bag, i.e. the warmest available, ice axe, crampons, down jacket and salopettes, prussic loops (a special loop which attaches to the rope and moves up, but not down, and is used as a foothold), karabiners and double boots. The boots proved to be a nightmare to find. Onesport boots have an inner and outer boot and are designed for maximum warmth and insulation. They are huge, heavy and cumbersome, but essential in the freezing temperatures of Antarctica. Vicky's problem was the size of her feet. She is a size five and because mountaineering is a male-dominated sport, Vicky simply could not find boots small enough. She contacted climbing shops all over the country, but only men's sizes were available and they were all too large. Eventually, Jagged Globe helped her to source a company who said they would find her the boots. Her colleagues in the office became accustomed to enormous boxes arriving for Vicky which contained the latest offering. She forgets how many times she tried boots on, found them too large and had to re-pack and return them. She was getting more and more concerned as the departure date drew closer: without the boots, the trip was off. And then, two days before she was due to leave, a box arrived containing a pair of man's size sevens. They were big and wide but, with two pairs of insoles and very thick socks, they would do. So, ten months after she had reached the summit of Aconcagua, she was ready to fly back to South America – but this time Chile would be a mere staging post on a much, much longer journey south.

She left on 18 November 1999. She expected to be away from work for at least three weeks, but bad weather in Antarctica was always a possibility and she knew she might be delayed a little longer. As things turned out, she would be away for more than five weeks. Over the preceding eighteen months, work at North of Scotland Water had been very hard and it had made huge demands on her time. In addition to all her other responsibilities, one of her main tasks had been to put in new staff terms and conditions. It had been a bruising period of reviews, assessments, talks, negotiations, more talks, threatened strike action, more negotiations and a final deal which the unions had voted to accept by an extremely narrow margin. 'I knew it wasn't going to be easy but, once I get the bit between my teeth, I won't give up' is how Vicky describes those months. Jim Finnie, who worked with her as Head of HR, admired her mental resilience and capacity for hard work. He was glad to be on *her* side of the table for negotiations. 'She can be a tough adversary who can really challenge you,' he says. She was going to need that tenacious spirit over the next few weeks.

* * * * *

Vicky's journey to the Antarctic began, appropriately enough, amid a light flurry of snow as her plane flew out of Inverness airport. The team for Vinson would be small, only herself, guide Tim Bird and the man she was to meet at Gatwick, Martin Wallen, the managing director of a family-owned paint business in Bolton. Like Vicky, Martin was an amateur climber, a lover of the hills, the outdoors and travelling to exotic destinations. In his teens he had gone with friends to the Lake District, Wales and Scotland, doing a little bit of rock climbing, but mostly hillwalking and scrambling, and then in his late twenties he started going on trekking trips abroad to Pakistan, India and Nepal. Antarctica had always attracted him because it is a frontier. Sixty per cent of the continent remains unexplored and although some 14,000 people visit each year by vessel, only 200 venture inland to explore the interior. The idea of going to a place still relatively untouched by man was deeply exciting, and so he saved and saved and, as he says, 'blew the whole lot' on the trip. He and Vicky spent the thirteen hours of the flight from London to Santiago (via Buenos Aires) chatting and finding out a little bit about each other and the climbs they had done. It is always a strange situation. Vicky knew she would be sharing a tent with this stranger for days on end and, although she wanted them to get to know each other on the journey out, she also wanted to save, as it were, some conversation for the weeks ahead.

I was thinking, 'Here we are. I don't know you from Adam, and we're sitting side by side on a plane and I'm terribly keen to ask you all sorts of things to get to know you, but there's going to be so much time in the next few weeks to get to know you, so I shouldn't rush it.' And I was also thinking, 'What will it be like on the way home? How well will we know each other? What experiences will we have shared?'

Vicky does not dwell on the risks of climbing high mountains. She accepts that there are dangers, but she trains to be fit, competent and self-reliant on the hill and she has respect for the environments she climbs in. Sitting on the plane to Santiago, she was filled with excitement, not fear; the thought that she and Martin might end up battling for their lives in an Antarctic storm never crossed her mind. She was simply focused on the moment, getting to know this stranger with whom she would be sharing her life for the next few weeks, and hoping that her experiences on Elbrus and Aconcagua, and her strength and fitness which she had continued to build up over the year, would equip her for the climb which lay ahead.

They spent a couple of days in Santiago, and then caught a flight to Punta Arenas, the port city at the southernmost tip of the Andes in Patagonia, on the western side of the Straits of Magellan. Punta Arenas is the best and largest port for thousands of miles, attracting ships from the South Atlantic fishing industry, Antarctic research vessels and tourist vessels bound for Tierra del Fuego and the Patagonian fjords and glaciers. Although there are many fine buildings dating from the wool boom of the nineteenth and early twentieth centuries, the city has the look of a frontier town: corrugated iron roofs painted red, blue and green under an endless sky and surrounded by thousands of miles of ocean. Vicky might have enjoyed it more if their stay had been just a couple of days, but because of bad weather in Antarctica the plane could not fly and they were stuck for nearly a week.

The first few days they spent exploring the city, getting to know some of the other climbing groups and travellers at the various hotels, and attending briefing sessions run by Adventure Network International (ANI), a company set up in 1985 to provide flights to Antarctica and trips to the South Pole and interior. The season for trekking and climbing in the Antarctic is short and there were around thirty people waiting at the hotel for their Hercules flight to ANI's base at Patriot Hills. There was a group of Greek climbers, bound for Vinson, and a team of American extreme skiers from Jackson Hole in Wyoming who were going to the Vinson Massif to film themselves climbing up and then snowboarding and skiing down the mountain. Also staying at a nearby hotel in Punta Arenas were the five British women who were bidding to become the first all-female British expedition to reach both the North and South Poles. They achieved their goal of the North Pole in 1997 and here they were, kicking their heels in Punta Arenas, waiting for the weather to improve so that they could embark on their

Vicky with her mum and dad at Luss
Highland Games, around 1959

With her dad and brother,
Brian, on holiday at
Ardnamurchan, around 1967

The family enjoying a
moment of madness!

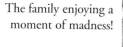

very young Vicky modelling a dressing
gown for her dad's childrenswear
business and . . .

her second attempt at a modelling career!
Everest Camp 2 – the outfit (minus the
boots!) to be worn on summit day

On top of Slioch – Vicky and friends
celebrate her last Munro in September 1996

The one pair of boots
that took her up all the
Munros (resoled three
times!)

Winter climbing in
the Cairngorms in
preparation for
Everest

The Priutt Hut with Elbrus in the background

View of Kilimanjaro

Celebrating at the summit of Kilimanjaro

The long walk-in to Base Camp –
Aconcagua, Argentina, December 1998

Vicky, Chris and Shirley on
the summit of Aconcagua,
Christmas Day 1998

Putting on crampons
Refugia Independenc
on Aconcagua

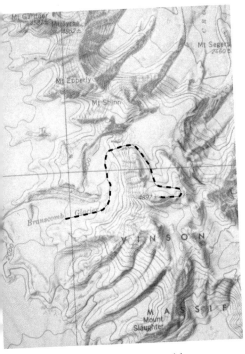

The route taken by Vicky and her team marked on a map of the Vinson Massif, Antarctica

Portering their own kit up to the top camp on Vinson

Looking back to Vinson Base Camp

Having just dug a foot pit at the entrance
to the tent in Antarctica

Running out of reading material – sharing
what was left!

Vicky found passport stamps
at Patriot Hills Camp and set
up shop stamping passports!

Martin freezing in -50 temperatures at the top camp on Vinson

Vicky on the summit of Vinson

View from the summit of Vinson looking down into the valleys behind

Downtown Talkeetna, Alaska
– the team flew from here to
the Base Camp of McKinley

Roped up, dragging sledges and picking their
way through the Kahiltna Glacier up to
14,000ft on McKinley

Vicky on the
summit of
McKinley

Celebrating the safe return to Base Camp on McKinley with a 'wee dram' –
Chris (left), Morris (centre), Vicky (right)

695-mile trek to the South Pole. Vicky and Martin used to go for drinks in the evening with some of the other folk heading for Antarctica, to sample the local cocktail called a pisco sour: clear brandy, lime juice, egg whites, syrup and bitters. The British explorer David Hempleman-Adams also sampled pisco sours on his way to climb Vinson and concluded that 'no man could drink three in a row'.

Vicky, Martin and Tim had been on a mammoth shopping expedition to the supermarket when they arrived and filled three trolleys to the brim with supplies. When it came to selecting sweet things to eat, they were a tad over-enthusiastic. 'We cleared them out of fruit cake,' says Martin. 'But it turned out to be a terrible choice. It all froze on the climb and I remember sitting in the freezing tent hacking through it and trying to thaw it under my arm!' Eventually, though, with shopping and sightseeing done, they grew fed up with pisco sours, daily weather reports, walking round the local cemetery for the tenth time and packing and re-packing their kit, so they hired a pick-up truck and drove to the Parque Nacional Torres del Paine which is famous for its stunning tall granite towers: high, strangely shaped mountains which look like a set of witch's teeth. The team did not climb there, but instead practised crevasse rescue in the big trees at the foot of the mountains. It is a very simple practice exercise: you put on your harness, climb a tree, attach the rope to the tree – and jump out. When you are dangling from the tree you practise the technique which will save your life if you fall down a crevasse: hoisting yourself up a rope by using a prussic loop which winds around the main rope and only moves up, not down. Vicky knew that in Antarctica they would be pulling sleds over miles of snow and ice, and over snow bridges which concealed deep crevasses. This was essential survival training.

When they returned to Punta Arenas, things were moving at last. The weather at Patriot Hills had improved, the plane was clear to fly and the backlog of people was diminishing. Vicky was thrilled to be on her way at last, even though it involved a four-and-a half-hour flight in the freezing-cold fuselage of a Hercules transporter plane, strapped into one of the temporary seats bolted to the floor for the flight, cocooned inside her down jacket and deafened by the roar of the engines. Their flight path took them over memorable landmarks, each an exotic evocation of centuries of history and exploration. They flew over Tierra del Fuego, the 'Land of Fire', as it was named by the Portuguese explorer Ferdinand Magellan, because he could see the campfires of the native Yahgan people burning along its shores; then they passed over the ocean south of Tierra del Fuego, the Drake Passage, and at around 60° South reached the winter limits of frozen seas. This area of ocean is called the Antarctic Convergence and marks the beginning of the territory which is governed by the Antarctic Treaty, an agreement first signed in 1959 and now encompassing more than thirty nations. Under the treaty no single country owns the continent, but simply administers a sector, and all pledge to promote international scientific cooperation, keep the zone de-militarised and pollution-free and set aside disputes over territorial sovereignty.

At 66° South the plane crossed the Antarctic Circle and flew over icebergs and ice shelves. The first sight of land proper was of two islands, Charcot and Alexander, lying in the Bellingshausen Sea. Mile after endless mile of ice spread out below as the plane flew on until, in the distance, Vicky could make out the peaks of the Ellsworth Mountains, the highest range in Antarctica. The northern group of mountains forms the Sentinel Range, home to six of the highest summits on the continent, including Vinson, highest of them all. At the southernmost edge of the Ellsworth Mountains the Patriot Hills rose into view and the plane began its descent towards a long sheet of blue ice which was the landing strip. The ice remains clear of snow because of the sheer force of the winds that roar down from the hills. The blue ice runway was breathtaking – a sea of granite-hard, frozen ripples and ridges. It ran for several kilometres, which was just as well since the Hercules could not use brakes on the ice. Vicky walked down the ramp and out of the back end of the plane and stepped cautiously on to the shiny, blue ice; it was not the cold that stunned her – it had been perishing in the plane – but the light and the vastness.

It was all blue sky, sunshine, whiteness. The light reflects off the pristine snow and ice, and the clarity of the atmosphere means that this intensely strong bright, white light suffuses everything. As I looked around I saw vastness and flatness. It was totally featureless, apart from the Patriot Hills which were a delight because they gave definition. I thought of the British women who were going to march across that flat, white, endless landscape for weeks and weeks.

Patriot Hills is the home of Adventure Network International's Base Camp, a temporary collection of tents about half a mile from the landing site which are erected for the summer season. The camp lies at 80° 19′ South latitude and 81° 16′ West longitude, 3,250 feet above sea level and 670 miles from the South Pole. It consisted of a big mess and cook tent, a storage area and a couple of toilet tents containing barrels with plastic bags. Everything goes into plastic bags and is removed. Every scrap of human litter and waste is taken away from the site, and all trekkers and climbers have to bag their waste and bring it back to Patriot Hills for transportation off the continent; as it all freezes almost immediately, this is not as awful as it sounds. The advice here is: leave nothing behind, apart from your footprints. There were also a couple of large accommodation tents for tourists. They were occupied by two American women who planned to do two trips with ANI – the first involved a flight to the South Pole (they'd already been to the North Pole) and, on the second, they were going to see the Emperor penguins on the Dawson-Lambton Glacier.

Vicky's team put up their tents about a hundred yards from the mess tent and settled themselves in for the night. However, because it was light for twenty-four hours, for most of the trip they operated according to their body clocks, and not the watch. They slept when they were tired. The next morning the weather was fine and the three teams who were going to Vinson were shuttled by Twin Otter plane to the Vinson Base Camp, a flight of about an hour and a quarter. Base Camp sits at 7,200 feet on the Branscomb Glacier and as soon as they landed Vicky, Martin and Tim erected their tents and started to build a curved 'modesty wall' of snow blocks a little way off which would afford some privacy for going to the loo. The Twin Otter, having made its final delivery, turned, sped across the ice and buzzed away into the empty blue sky. They would not see it again until Tim radioed on their return from Vinson. It was an unforgettable moment.

We watched the plane take off. There was no big runway. It just raced off, dropped off this shelf we were on, lifted into the sky and got smaller and smaller. It was a beautiful day, completely still. The noise of the plane got less and less, less and less. We just stood there in a line, in silence, watching our lifeline disappearing. And the immensity of where we were, the overwhelming vastness of the place, settled over us as the tiny plane disappeared. It looked like a seagull at one stage, and then it was gone. There were no birds, nothing green; there was just white snow and ice. After the plane had gone we still stood there in silence, in a line. I was thinking, 'This is it. What happens if something goes wrong? If a storm comes in, we'll be marooned here.' But I was also thinking, 'How beautiful this is. What a privilege to stand here in this world where so few people have ever been.' I'll never forget that feeling.

More than any of the Seven Summits, climbing Vinson was not really about the climb itself: for Vicky it was much more about the unique experience of the place and the environment. The immensity. The cold, a cold unlike any other she would ever experience. The isolation. The severe beauty of snow and ice and sky. The thrilling realisation that if she took a few steps to the right or left of the route, or if she climbed to the top of that ridge over there, she would probably be standing where no human had ever stood before. There was a deep, wonderful magic and an ever-present threat in this white wilderness. It was a privilege to be there precisely because it was both dangerous and infinitely precious.

The Vinson Massif lay before them, by way of a five-and-a-half mile trek through the Branscomb Glacier which gently rises 2,000 feet to the base of the Icefall; from the Icefall there is a steep climb to the High Camp (12,140 feet) on a col between Vinson and neighbouring Mount Shinn. From there the route crosses a slope of hard, boiler-plate ice and a short steep climb to the summit ridge. The mountain was named after Carl Vinson, a congressman who campaigned for many years for the US government to support the exploration of Antarctica. It was first sighted by US Navy pilots during an aerial reconnaissance flight in 1957, and not climbed until 1966 when the American Antarctic Mountaineering Expedition spent forty days climbing six peaks in the range. Many years later, in 1983, Dick Bass became the first person to climb Vinson as part of a Seven Summits challenge.

Now it was Vicky's turn. Ahead lay a journey of five to nine days, depending on the weather. They loaded up their plastic sleds, or *pulks*, and set off on the long trek to Camp 1. These first few days were basically extended trudges, pulling and carrying considerable weights.

We were roped up because we were going over glacier and snow, across snowbridges which concealed crevasses. And our sleds were roped to the person behind and it was their responsibility to control it. But when we set off it was along the side of a hill, so the pulks were difficult to control and slid down at an angle. You have no idea how difficult it is to pull a sled which is askew and lying at an angle behind you. We had crampons and walking poles, and they were vital to keep balance. I was carrying a heavy pack which probably weighed about 30–40 lb: that's an 80-litre pack which is mammoth compared to what you would take for climbing Munros. We were carrying, or pulling, everything we would need – tents, food, fuel, sleeping kit, extra food, extra clothing. You don't know how long you're going to be out, if the weather is bad. It was a heavy day, that first day.

The next day they encountered their first bout of bad weather. The wind whipped up the snow, the skies became leaden and it was impossible to see the way ahead. Tim navigated by compass, but as they were travelling over terrain riddled with crevasses, it was nerve-racking progress. They holed up until the weather improved and moved on to Camp 2. But the waiting time had been well spent. Tim was an extremely experienced climber and guide who had also worked for the British Antarctic Survey, and he had a great deal of knowledge to share with Vicky and Martin. Much of what she learned from Tim was invaluable to Vicky when it came to climbing the other mountains.

I learned a heck of a lot from him about what you would call the domestic side of climbing: the packing of your rucksack;, the order you should put things in; what you should have on your harness and where you clip it for ease of access. He just gently taught us these kinds of things. Winterising your zips, for example: that's when you tie bits of string on to the ends of zips so that you can get hold of it when you're wearing thick gloves. He also told us about digging a little trench in front of the tent, in the space between the inner tent and flysheet, so that you could unzip the inner tent and sit there with your legs in the trench, like a seat. That was so much more comfortable than having to sit hunched up inside. These were all little tips which were hugely useful.

At the end of each long day's climb they would pitch camp. It sounds a fairly straightforward procedure, but it took hours. It wasn't just a case of putting up the tents. They had to build an ice wall around them to shelter them from the wind and weather; if a storm blew up, without this extra protection the tents would be plucked from the ice and disappear. Constructing these walls was back-breaking and time-consuming work. Tim was the most experienced at cutting the big blocks of ice and snow with the snow saw, and then Vicky and Martin would trim them, haul them into position and build the wall, three or four feet high. They would put up the tents first, and then build the wall around them. The trenches inside the fly sheet also had to be dug, and then enormous amounts of snow had to be gathered for melting. The stove was lit as soon as the tents were up, and it would burn for hours, giving them enough water for drinking and cooking. If they weren't all exhausted by that time, someone would go out and build the modesty wall, but that was low on the list of priorities when you were cold, tired and hungry.

And there they would sit, crouched in their tents, resting through the Antarctic summer night which is simply a continuation of the day. Their tents were two tiny bright orange pimples on a vast white desert; in the distance the great white upward sweep of Vinson, Mount Shinn and the peaks and valleys of the Sentinel Range; above them the immensity of the sky. No sound, except the ever-present wind. Two other climbing parties were in the vicinity but, for Vicky, the great exhilaration was that the three of them were essentially alone in this breathtaking landscape.

The landscape was breathtaking – and so was the cold. This is a cold which freezes the hairs in your nostrils and burns the back of your throat when you take your first deep breath in the morning. It is a cold where you simply do not venture out without being covered from head to toe. While they were on the move, they did not wear their huge down jackets because they would become too warm with exertion and the last thing you want to do is to sweat and have to start taking clothes off. In this climate the body cools down very quickly. You don't really want to stop for anything, even to pee. It was, of course, much more complicated for Vicky than the men.

> It's a real palaver when you're roped up to each other, to your pulk and to the pulk in front. You've also got a harness on, and big boots and crampons. I had to find a way of pulling everything down and at the same time not take my harness off. And you've got gloves on, too. It really was a mammoth effort – difficult and annoying. And, of course, you got colder and colder the longer it took.

The higher they went, the colder it became. High Camp was at the top of a steep slope of snow, on the edge of a col. They had left their pulks at Camp 3 and now faced an arduous climb, carrying all their kit on their backs, through deep snow, heaving their legs out of deep drifts. As they climbed, Vicky's right hand, the one holding her ice axe, began to get very, very cold. She knew something was wrong. Her fingers were numb and she feared she was getting frostbite. Tim immediately took charge and massaged them until, eventually, the circulation began to return; the hot pain of the blood reaching her fingers again was a great relief. But it was a warning: Vicky had been wearing double gloves, but the circulation had slowed up in one hand because it was tightly gripped round her ice axe. Her hand did not even need to be exposed to the cold.

That night at High Camp, at 12,188 feet, was the coldest Vicky has ever been in her life. It was an intense, frightening cold, impossible to compare to anything at home on the hills of Scotland, or high up on Aconcagua.

It wasn't cold. It was absolutely freezing. A tiny bit of water had got into the fuel pipe of the stove and frozen, so it wouldn't light. We tried and tried. You have to have a stove to melt ice for drinking and we were all seriously wondering what we would do if it didn't light. Eventually we unfroze the pipe, but it kept cutting out. We managed to get warm water, but that was all. There were three of us in a two-man tent, for warmth. Martin is a big man – over six feet tall – and we all squashed in together. Somehow Martin got the middle and Tim and I were out on either side, and we were all rammed up against each other, but I still froze. It was seriously – I mean, seriously – cold and I was unable to get warm, no matter what. I couldn't sleep at all and it really was a horrible night.

Relief came when it was time to leave camp and get moving again. This final push would see them climb nearly 4,000 feet to the summit at 16,067 feet. It is an exposed route and subject to high winds, the majority of it along the Vinson Summit glacier, across an ice slope and up the rocky, summit ridge. Vicky remembers it as a long, hard trudge. Steep steps on the shoulders, then flatter bits, then more steep slopes. They had left everything at High Camp and were carrying only their daypacks, but at that altitude, and through deep snow, she was feeling it.

I remember on the last rise up to the summit – maybe 500 feet or so – it turned into hard ice, what you call boiler-plate ice. It wasn't a steep wall or anything like that, but you really had to kick in hard with your crampons to get a grip, and it had never struck me before that a crampon could slip on ice. It was very hard work, and I remember thinking, 'Gosh, this is a cruel thing to have so near the top!' But then we were at the summit and it was stunning. I could see for miles – mountains, flat valleys, vast stretches of ice sheet. I remember looking down into a big valley and thinking, 'I wonder if anyone's ever been there before?' The vastness was so overpowering, the sheer size and magnitude. Of course people had been where I was standing; but what about a few feet away?

There is a glorious picture of Vicky standing on the summit of Vinson, her right arm aloft, holding her ice axe. The sun is behind her, casting a shadow across the snow, which looks more like a vast, pointed heap of sugar than a mountain of ice. Behind her the sky is streaked with clouds. There are footprints in the snow, leading up the slope to where she is standing. There is nothing else in the picture. Just a figure, alone on the top of a mountain. Vicky knows that people have stood where she stood, and that more will come – unless the carbon footprint left by tourist flights to the Antarctic becomes less acceptable in these times of fear and concern about global warming. But Antarctica covers 5.4 million square miles and most of it is still unexplored and untouched; perhaps those unknown and unvisited miles include the valley away down there in the sea of ice and snow, on the other side of that mountain. Perhaps.

Back at Vinson Base Camp, the weather began to change and they had to wait for a couple of days for the Twin Otter to come and pick them up. The Greek climbers and American extreme skiers were there, too, and the three groups shared a mess tent. They played cards to pass the time and cooked together. As usual, the Mediterranean food was the tastiest because the Greeks – incidentally, the first Greeks to climb in Antarctica – had brought proper food with them: not the beef jerky and processed survival food the Americans carried, or the instant porridge the British had brought, but fresh garlic and olive oil, all the way from Greece. They boiled up water with fried garlic and cooked a makeshift soup for everyone.

By the time they got back to Patriot Hills the weather was still changeable. Vicky cannot remember exactly when the storm broke, but at some point she and Martin had gone back to their tent to rest – whether it was at 'night' or not, Vicky can't remember – and that was when the winds suddenly increased and the area was engulfed in a huge storm. ANI staff who had been working at Patriot Hills for several seasons said later that they were the worst winds they had ever seen. The temperature dropped to around -50°C and the winds reached 100 m.p.h. Inside their tent, Vicky and Martin could not hear each other speak above the screaming and roaring.

I was on the windward side of the tent, and Martin was on the leeward. The wind was battering against the side of the tent which was bending over as the flexible poles took the strain. The entrance was at my feet, and the tent was slamming and bulging into my side as I lay there. The wind was so fierce that it was driving the snow up into the narrow gap between the flysheet and the tent, and the weight of snow was beginning to collapse the tent. I was hammering with my fists against the inside fabric, trying to dislodge the snow, but it was a losing battle. I was shouting at Martin and he at me, but the noise of the storm was so horrifically loud that we simply could not communicate – and he was only a foot away from me. The wind was a roar, a powerful, deafening, endless roar.

The winds were tearing along the ice sheet from the South Pole, gaining speed and intensity as they raced towards the coast, driving down from the Patriot Hills and slamming straight into the group of tents. Martin and Vicky knew that if they stayed in the tent they were in mortal danger, so they motioned to each other that they would have to get out and try to find their way the 100 yards or so to the big mess and storage tents. In the confined, heaving tent they struggled to put on their heavy boots, down jackets, double gloves, neoprene face masks and goggles. Not an inch of flesh could be unprotected. Then they wriggled into their harnesses, and, last of all before they ventured into the storm, they put on their crampons and roped up.

They fumbled to unzip the outer tent, inched their way through and braced themselves for the full brunt of the elements. The wind slammed into them like a giant battering ram, and they were engulfed by the blizzard of snow whipped up by the storm. It was a white-out. They simply could not see beyond a yard in front of them. They crawled on hands and knees out of the battered tent, and promptly tumbled into a pit. Such was the force of the storm, that the wind had gouged out great bowls of snow and blasted craters all over the campsite. Martin remembers briefly trying to use the compass on his watch, but it was useless; he couldn't see to read it, and he realised that, of course, being a watch from the northern hemisphere, it wouldn't have worked anyway in the Antarctic. Only a few feet from the tent, the two of them were in serious trouble.

Falling into the hole was enough to disorientate us and make us lose our sense of direction. We couldn't turn back because we knew the tent was going to be trashed, so we had to keep going. But which direction? We were stumbling and falling into pits. We had made the trip from tent to mess tent many times before the storm, so we knew which way to turn when we left the tent, but with the pits and the white-out conditions we were effectively blind. We knew that if we missed the mess tent by only a few feet we would crawl out into the wilderness and die. It was like looking for a needle in a haystack.

We had 360 degrees around us and we could have gone in any direction and missed the tent. It was horrific.

Looking back now, both Vicky and Martin know how close they came to dying. Martin remembers the snow battering across his goggles; it was impossible to wipe them clear because the wind was relentless. The landscape was completely featureless, sky and snow tumbled together in the freezing wind. Neither Martin nor Vicky has any idea how long they fought their way through the storm. They cannot remember if they crawled one behind the other, or shoulder to shoulder. At the time, Vicky says she was aware that their chances of survival were slim, and Martin knew very well that if they missed the mess tent they would be swallowed up by the vast Antarctic emptiness; but they both drove these thoughts to the back of their minds as they forced themselves not to panic, and to work as a team. They could not communicate, but they were anchored to each other by the rope in the midst of the raging chaos around them, and that gave them heart. They kept close, they kept going, they trusted to their initial instinct about the direction of the mess tent, and they didn't give up. And, in the end, they did find the needle in the haystack. They miraculously stumbled against the side of the mess tent, inched their way round to the end and found the way in. When they saw, several days later, that the storm had thrown massive quantities of snow in great drifts against the mess tent and partially buried it – and the mess tent was at least ten feet high – it seemed even more incredible that they ever found it. They had been very, very lucky. And they had kept their heads. Vicky believes that she and Martin shared the temperament to cope, and Martin, reflecting on the Vicky he came to know on that trip, summed her up as 'a pretty tough girl. There didn't seem to be much that wound her up. She's a cool cookie.'

They had survived, but the storm was not over. Everyone

else in the camp had either already been in the mess tent or had managed to get there, and for the next five days about twenty or so people were marooned while the storm blew itself out. People slept where they could – on the floor of the storage tents, in corners of the mess tent. There was no communication possible with the outside world because the radio was down, so no one knew when the Hercules would be able to come and get them.

However, there was no shortage of supplies and the ANI staff made sure that everyone was well fed and watered. The Patriot Hills camp is completely dismantled at the end of the each season and non-perishable goods are stored in huge underground caves dug into the snow; by this stage in the season there was a vast supply of wine in the stores, and over the next few days the marooned tourists and climbers proceeded to drink their way through the entire lot. There was little else to do except eat (three hearty meals a day, plus afternoon tea and cake), drink, play cards and chess, read, chat and sleep. Vicky was now well past her planned return date to Scotland and she began to worry about her mother: Was she running out of food? Was she worrying about Vicky? Was she all right on her own? When communications were restored a few days later, she managed to phone her mother on a very crackly, faint line. Her mother was absolutely thrilled to be speaking to Vicky in Antarctica. 'How is the weather, Vick? Are you having a nice time? I can't believe you're at the South Pole!' Vicky told her the plane had been a bit delayed, but everything was fine and she would be back by Christmas.

The call to work had to be made as well. It was a fantastic excuse, though. None of your 'I've got a sore throat' or 'I've got to wait in for the plumber' – 'I'm marooned in the Antarctic by the worst storm for years, and I'll be late coming back' has a definite ring to it.

It was an odd collection of travellers who were stuck with

each other's company for four days. The Americans got itchy feet very quickly and came up with all kinds of ploys to keep themselves amused; when the wind abated enough for people to go outside, they built two snow walls, embedded a ski pole across the top and did pull-ups. One morning they trekked off to look at an old wrecked plane which lay some distance away. The Greeks found a children's book which described how to build an igloo, so a big group of people spent hours in the snow, cutting the snow blocks and constructing a rather fine one. There was an American couple, a mother and son, who were on a trip to the South Pole. There was a Belgian man who was planning to cross Antarctica with a friend, wind surfing on skis. When the weather eased, he practised his technique on the ice, shooting in this direction and that, falling over and picking himself up, to the amused concern of the others. Vicky cannot remember whether the trip was ever completed. The two American women, who had gone to see the Emperor penguins on the Dawson-Lambton Glacier, were extremely unhappy about their trip home being so delayed and they were still complaining about the fact that a part of the ice shelf on which the penguins were to be found had broken off and floated away, carrying the penguins with it.

As the days wore on, tempers became frayed and people were desperate to get away. Vicky tried to spread a little light and happiness one day when she pulled out a box from under a chair in the mess tent and found an inkpad and set of stampers. They turned out to be passport stamps for Antarctica, so Vicky gaily started stamping her own and other people's passports. She had already gathered a queue of people and was happily at work when someone questioned whether it was actually illegal to stamp your own passport. It turned out later that it was fine, but that was the end of that game. Vicky still has the 'home-made' stamps in an old passport, a quirky little reminder of those surreal days stranded in the Antarctic.

7

THE HARDEST JOURNEY
MOUNT McKINLEY

As soon as Vicky got back from Antarctica she set about tackling the backlog at work. She was working long hours during the week, as well as starting to plan and train for her next expedition to summit number 5, Mount McKinley in Alaska, the highest mountain in North America. And every Friday evening she drove down as usual from Inverness to Balquhidder – stopping to buy shopping on the way – to spend the weekend with her mother. She was sometimes so tired that she'd phone her mother on a Friday evening to say she'd be there on the Saturday morning instead. One Friday evening in January 2000 she phoned Maureen to say exactly that, but her mother sounded rather upset and said, 'Oh, do you not love me any more?' Vicky did what she often did when her mother was a little frail or confused. She reassured her and suggested something to do and to look forward to.

> 'Of course I love you, mum. We'll have a good weekend together. I'd love to have some lentil soup for lunch. We can make it together but could you soak the lentils overnight?'

Her mother was much cheered at the end of the phone call and said she'd do the lentils and see Vicky the next day. But on Saturday morning Tommy Macgregor looked out of his living room, across the road to Maureen's cottage, and saw that the curtains were still drawn. Tommy and his wife, Betty, had known Tom and Maureen Jack since they'd moved to Balquhidder in 1985. 'They were a lovely couple,' Tommy says, with a smile. He has fond memories of one winter when the glen was smothered in snow and the driveway to the Jacks' cottage was completely blocked. He remembers seeing Tom digging through three or four feet of snow so that he could get his car out of the garage. So Tommy got out his spade and started shovelling from the top of the drive. They met in the middle, shook hands and Tom said, 'Come on inside. That calls for a dram!' After Tom Jack died, Betty and Maureen used to meet for a cup of coffee in each other's houses and in later years, when Maureen was no longer able to drive, Tommy used to go into Callander twice a week for her shopping. On a Sunday morning at twelve o'clock he would bring her newspaper, and stay for an hour. He would have a dram, and Maureen would have a sherry.

So when Betty and Tommy saw that Maureen's curtains were still drawn that January morning, they were concerned. When Tommy walked over to the cottage he could hear a tap running in the kitchen, but there was no reply when he knocked. Eventually he managed to get into the house where he found Maureen unconscious on the living room floor. By the time Vicky arrived her mother had been taken to Stirling Royal Hospital and was in a coma. She'd had a massive stroke. Vicky has played the scene in her mind countless times and she believes that after the phone call her mother went straight to the kitchen cupboard, took out the packet of lentils, put on the cold tap to soak them – and then had her stroke. Vicky thinks she staggered from the kitchen and tripped on the step down into the living room, falling badly and lying unconscious overnight.

For five days Vicky sat by her mother's bedside in hospital, holding her hand. Over and over again the thought kept repeating in her head: If I'd only been there. Why had she not just driven down that night, exhausted as she was? She could not bear to think of her mother lying through the night. The doctor reassured her that Maureen would have known very little about it, and that it would have made no difference if Vicky had been there, but that did not help her grief or numb her feelings of guilt. She had always been there for her mother, she loved being with her, and yet, for one night, she had not been there. During the days at the hospital, waiting and sitting, time went out of shape, and everything which had been clear and familiar was changed. The figure in the bed was Maureen, but she was not her mum anymore. Her real mum was inside Vicky, cradled in her heart, alive and free in her mind. Maureen Jack died in hospital, on 26 January 2000. She was 76.

Vicky had been so close to her mother that she felt broken in two. Maureen had been her best friend, the person in the world who perhaps best understood her. The one who had delighted in everything Vicky did, and encouraged her to embrace life and take on challenges. She had been an inspiration and Vicky was bereft without her.

I was numb. I was so devastated. Mum was everything, and she took up so much time as well, in a nice way, that my whole life stopped. I thought of McKinley – that was my plan, to do McKinley in May – and I said, 'I've just got to go and do it, I've got to do it. Mum would have wanted me to do it.' You know how you make these stories in your mind. Because if I had cancelled McKinley, then what would I have done? I'd have thrown myself into work, but I'd have had nothing else to do outwith work. Whereas this way I could batter myself with training and run away from the problem because it was so overwhelming I couldn't think it through.

Vicky coped with her grief in the way anyone who has experienced loss will understand: she picked herself up, gathered in all her pain and sadness, and turned it into a fierce energy directed at something specific and consuming: climbing Mount McKinley. She was too strong a person to collapse and give way. Instead she focused all her attention on what would be the severest challenge of the Seven Summits so far.

Lying just south of the Arctic Circle in Alaska, at 20,320 feet (6,194 metres) Mount McKinley is one of the coldest mountains in the world. It has a reputation for bad weather and is considered the most difficult of the Seven Summits after Everest, because it combines altitude and cold. 'If you can get to the top of Mount McKinley,' Vicky was told by climbing friends, 'you can get to the top of Everest.' McKinley is a massive mountain, seriously cold and demanding of stamina and strength, and it has claimed the lives of many, many climbers. Vicky had already had a taste of altitude on the 23,000-feet Aconcagua in South America, she'd experienced the cold of Antarctica and now she was going to contend with both. She would also be carrying very large amounts of kit. In addition to the 40–50lb rucksack on her back, she would be dragging a sledge weighing between 100 and 120lb, far heavier than the pulk she'd pulled across the ice in Antarctica. And she would be wearing snow-shoes for the first time in her life.

Vicky had a very simple training plan: carry heavier and heavier loads up hills, do as many Munros as possible and generally push herself to the point of exhaustion. As well as going to the gym after work practically every night, she devised some fiendishly hard training methods of her own. In order to get used to carrying heavy loads on her back, she filled her rucksack with telephone directories. She began doing this when she was training for Aconcagua and Vicky carrying telephone directories was to become her trademark image in the newspapers. She carried more and more of them until that day with her friends Jean and Shona, when she climbed the South Shiel Ridge with sixteen phone books on her back! The pain in her shoulders and back where the straps cut into the flesh was severe, as was the strain on her legs coming down, but she kept telling herself that she might have to endure far worse on McKinley.

Her other training technique was designed to simulate the sledge which she would be dragging over glaciers and snowy terrain. She had a good friend in Forres called Ron Swanson, an experienced hillwalker who for many years had been an instructor with Outward Bound, and he designed a special contraption for her. He had read somewhere about somebody using a tyre for training, so he got an old large-sized motor tyre, drilled a couple of holes in it and put some wire through; then Vicky clipped two karabiners on to the wires, attached one end of a rope to those and the other to her climbing harness. On a typical training session Vicky would fill the tyre with rocks, put on her rucksack which was stuffed to the gunwales with phone books, and trek around the forestry tracks of Aviemore, hauling the homemade sled behind her, generally in the dark because all her training during the week took place after work.

It was along Loch Morlich side, on the way up to the ski lift, along the forestry tracks there. I had a head torch so that I could see in the dark. What an idiot I felt, climbing out of the car, putting on the rucksack with the sixteen telephone directories and then this car tyre contraption! It was quite a long, gentle uphill for about a mile and then a short, steep hill up to the telegraph pole at the top. I used to hate that steep bit and would think, 'I'm not going to make it'. But I pushed on because I told myself, 'If I don't get to the top, I'm not going to get to the top of McKinley.'

Ron never actually saw Vicky using his tyre contraption but he has been hillwalking with her plenty of times. 'She's at home on the hills,' he says. 'She's very strong and fit and capable.' He is clearly very fond of her and admires her tenacity and determination, which are often masked by a natural modesty – he says he had no idea she was doing the Seven Summits until after she had already climbed two of them. He knew all about McKinley, though, and what a tough challenge it would be. Vicky explained to him why she needed the special tyre device, and he knew how hard she was training. She was very clear that this mountain was going to be very tough, because of altitude, cold and the amount of kit she would have to drag, so she had to trust that her careful preparation and training would be sufficient.

I didn't know anyone who had done McKinley, so I didn't know how fit you had to be, but I did know you couldn't have porters and I knew that was going to be a heck of a job. So I just decided to use telephone directories and the tyre contraption. I honestly had no idea how heavy my pack or sledge were going to be so I thought, 'Well, I'm going to pile on these phone directories and rocks until I can't stand! And if that's not sufficient, I just need to come home!' But I knew that, come hell or high water, I was going to get to the top. I never thought, 'What happens if I die on the way?' Because I think you wouldn't go and do these things if you ever had these thoughts.

* * * * *

The little four-seater plane took off from Talkeetna, a small railroad town about 115 miles north of Anchorage, Alaska, and buzzed over meandering rivers, miles of dense forests and gleaming swathes of flooded mosquito swamps. It was May 2000, and Vicky was many weeks and thousands of miles away from home. The evenings spent dragging the make-shift training tyre filled with rocks around the forestry tracks of Aviemore were far behind her, and Mount McKinley lay ahead of her, somewhere in this vast country. She peered out of the tiny window of the plane.Now and again a tiny house appeared in the middle of nowhere, alone and dwarfed in the massive landscape. They flew up a valley between two hills and directly in front of them was a high col. The plane seemed to be heading straight for it. Cramped in her tiny seat at the back, Vicky thought, 'That's it. We're finished.' At the very last moment the plane rose up and hopped over the col. They had just navigated their way through the worryingly named One Shot Pass. Vicky asked the pilot where the name came from, although she had a pretty good idea. Apparently, there is a thermal current which lurks around the hills and the way to catch it is to fly straight at the col where, at the last minute, you are lifted up and over. If the thermal is not there for some reason, or the pilot doesn't steer the correct course, well, hence the name. At any rate, they were over the pass, and gradually the trees and swamps gave way to snow and glaciers. As the plane began to lose height, Doug Geeting, the pilot, pointed out a great mass in the distance, surrounded by rocky outcrops and covered in ice: there it was at last – Mount McKinley, the highest mountain in North America, which the native Inuit people of Alaska call Denali, the 'High One'.

Doug Geeting's plane landed, on skis, on the massive Kahiltna Glacier where many tents were already pitched and Vicky and Chris Boggon clambered out, collected the luggage and made their way over to the main tent to register with the mountain rangers and confirm that their party was going on the hill. Meanwhile, Doug had taken off again on his second trip to collect the other two members of the team and the rest of the luggage. Vicky and Chris, an engineer from Godalming whom Vicky had met on the trip to Aconcagua, had flown from London to Seattle, where they met Morris Kittleman, an American climber and guide whom Chris knew. Then all three had flown on to Anchorage where they collected the final member of the team, Eric Blakely, a television reporter from the Channel Islands who was also attempting the Seven Summits. This was Eric's they should buy and how much, until eventually Morris took charge and said that they'd need a high-carbohydrate, high-fat diet because it was going to be cold and they would be burning lots and lots of calories. So they bought what appeared to Vicky to be ridiculous numbers of bagels – plain, sesame seed, blueberry, cinnamon – a whole trolleyful of bagels. Then great mounds of streaky, fatty bacon were added, and kilo upon kilo of butter. Crisps, powdered milk, biscuits, sweets, a few boil-in-the-bag meals, they all went into the trolleys. When Vicky suggested buying nuts, the idea was immediately pooh-poohed by Morris on the grounds that they would be too heavy, but Vicky insisted and said she would just buy a small amount and would carry them herself if necessary. Morris relented and Vicky recalls with a wicked laugh that, from that moment on, she never saw a single nut on the entire trip. 'He ate them all!' On the other hand, Morris was proved absolutely right about the bagels. They served the group well (although Vicky loathed the way they were cooked, deep-fried in butter, and found them very difficult to stomach), and they brought back only one packet with them from the mountain.

With all the supplies bought, they drove from Anchorage to Talkeetna for the flight to Mount McKinley. From the arrival camp near the airstrip where Doug Geeting's tiny plane landed, it is a long and arduous walk-in to Camp 1 at 8,000 feet. They trekked 1,000 feet down Heartbreak Hill on to the Kahiltna Glacier which climbs steadily to 14,000 feet. That first day turned out to be a nightmare for Vicky. Dragging her massive sledge, carrying around 50lb on her back and battling with the unwieldy snowshoes was an enormous strain. Everyone found it tough. They were carrying enormous loads of all their kit and supplies and Chris admits he didn't enjoy the first three days at all. It was extremely hard work. When they eventually got to the bottom of Heartbreak Hill and stopped for a few minutes, Vicky fell over. And couldn't get up again. They were all roped to one another's sledges so that each person was not only pulling their own sledge but was responsible for making sure the sled in front didn't run into the heels of the person in front. While they were momentarily stopped, Chris had pulled slightly on Vicky's rope and instinctively she took a step backwards, tripped over her snowshoe and fell down in a heap. Try as she might, weighed down with her rucksack, she simply didn't have the strength to stand up again. No one in her team could help her because they were all roped and kitted up, so eventually two other climbers who had taken off their packs for a rest came over, smiling, and pulled her to her feet.

Vicky smiled as well, but it was a serious blow to her confidence. How on earth could she climb a 20,000-foot mountain when she couldn't even stand up with her pack? In the pit of her stomach she felt sick at the possibility that this mountain, this challenge she'd set herself, might be beyond her capabilities.

I kept thinking, 'What am I doing here? I can't go back because someone's going to have to come back with me, and two people can't go on on their own. We've started on this journey, but only just. I've got to give it my best shot and go as far as I possibly can'. But I actually thought just then – and for the first and only time, I think – 'This is beyond my reach'.

But she said nothing, and nothing was said by the men. Not even that night in the tent with Chris when it would have been normal to mention it, to say that it was a horrible moment, or perhaps to laugh about it, if she could. But talking about her feelings is not Vicky's way, especially not on that trip where it took all her focus and concentration to keep herself mentally strong.

I don't do that. I don't like people who whinge and complain that they're not well or don't like what they're doing – unless,

110

of course, it's a serious issue. Because I think it has a negative effect on the morale of a whole team. And I think, too, I was so emotionally fragile that I never spoke about Mum when I was away. Chris knew what was going on, but he never raised it. I think he was right because I was so lonely and isolated anyway that, if someone had come and put their arm around me, I would have crumpled. No one had been there for me at that horrible, horrible time of my life from January right through to May, and for someone to close that horrendous chasm which was there – I don't think I could have coped.

It took three days to get up to 14,000 feet on the glacier, trekking over terrain where crevasses hidden beneath a layer of snow are a constant and nerve-racking danger. The glacier runs up to a steep face, an ice wall, where you leave the sledges and begin to climb the mountain proper. Vicky particularly remembers the loos at the big 14,000-foot camp. They were built over a crevasse, on top of planks of wood. A cylindrical plastic container with no top or bottom was secured over a gap, with a loo seat covered with polystyrene on top. It's so cold that you'd stick to the seat otherwise. Bliss! The comfort of just being able to sit down! There were two of those ingenious loos, but they were just a few yards apart and not shielded in any way from the rest of the world. The view from the seat was tremendous. There you were, sitting on a huge platform of white snow and ice in the bright sunshine, under a clear blue sky, looking out towards a mass of mountains in the distance and Mount Foraker in the foreground. The problem was that the seat was also in full view of the next person! There were very few women in the camp so, for a little privacy, Vicky would try to wait until both seats were unoccupied, but that proved impossible. It's a short, busy climbing season on McKinley and there were a lot of male climbers. So she just had to get on with it:

How do you play this, with a guy on the seat a few feet away? It's such a palaver to get your layers of trousers down. And you sit down eventually and think, 'Do I say hello?' It's just the two of you on two thrones sitting on a plateau of well-trodden snow above a crevasse. It's just the funniest feeling. So I felt I *had* to talk! 'Hello. It's a nice view, isn't it?'

They spent three days at that camp because of bad weather, and all the time Vicky was steeling herself for the next stage, hoping she'd be able to cope and not let the team or herself down. Early in the morning they left the sledges and some kit at the camp and set out for the headwall. Up a steep slope for about a quarter of a mile, and there it was, with a fixed rope attached. It took about an hour and a half to climb the ice wall and the team used a jumar to get up the fixed rope. This is a device which you clip on to a rope and which slides up, but doesn't slide down. It's very, very hard work, jumaring up a wall with a heavy pack because you're not supposed to be putting any weight on the fixed rope, but rather using it to support you, while you climb up with your feet and legs. They made one trip to the top, with half of the kit and supplies, and then descended. It was on the second ascent that things began to go wrong for Vicky. She was going quite slowly, behind Morris, who was strong and powerful and very experienced in this kind of climbing. Vicky still doesn't really know what happened, but she remembers that Morris began to throw back comments over his shoulder, telling her to hurry up and get her act together, making her feel as if she shouldn't be there – and suddenly, halfway up the ice wall, she simply burst into tears. There she was, 15,000 feet up on Mount McKinley, leaning into the ice wall, crying her heart out, Chris and Eric below her, craning their necks to try and see what was going on and, behind them, a queue of other climbers making their way up the rope. Above Vicky, Morris stopped climbing and stared down at her in consternation, but she couldn't stop crying. She leant her head against the ice and sobbed uncontrollably. Somehow she pulled herself together and got to the top of the wall, on to the shoulder of the mountain where they were to climb up the ridge to the top camp at 17,500 feet. But shortly after they began the ridge, Vicky realised she couldn't make it and said, 'I'm sorry, I can't go on any further'.

Mentally I couldn't go on because I was so upset. You don't just collapse and cry halfway up an ice face and then be strong and determined and spring out of it and on you go. And I wasn't crying about Morris. He couldn't really have upset me like that – I'd normally brush it off. I think I was probably crying for Mum, and that opened up all the emotional bit, and it's very hard to pull yourself back into this straitjacket again, and I couldn't manage it.

Vicky felt very guilty about stopping where they did, on a very exposed position on the ridge, because Morris was worried about a storm coming and blowing the tents off the mountain. But the weather held and the next morning they set off again. When they reached the top camp the three men returned to the previous night's camp for another load of luggage and Vicky single-handedly dug two platforms for the two tents, and had one tent erected by the time they came back. The men could hardly believe their eyes.

Vicky recovered from the drama and strain of the day before, but the rest of the climb didn't produce the same exhilaration as other ascents, that life-affirming sense of overcoming the obstacles, of pitting herself against herself and the physical challenge of the mountain. Morris was keeping a very sharp eye on her, and she was out of sorts and not feeling confident. On the day of the summit attempt it was bitterly cold. They were crossing a big plateau called the football field, just below the final ridge, and Vicky's goggles steamed up and then froze inside so she wasn't seeing well. She thinks she staggered once or twice and when they got to the beginning of the summit ridge, Morris told her she was to go no further. He believed she was suffering from the altitude. Chris, too, had been concerned about her and agreed with Morris. Vicky remembers the conversation with Morris:

'You're not going on, Vicky.'
  'Why not?'
  'You're all over the place. You've got problems, you're never going to make it to the top. This is ridiculous. It's really steep and we've got hours to go. You're never going to make it.'
  'I am going to make it.'
  'I'm going to make you turn back.'
  'You can't make me turn back. I'm fine.'
  'Then why are you staggering all over the place?'
  'Because I can't see!'

Morris was well within his rights to turn Vicky back if he thought it was dangerous for her and the team to go any further, and Vicky would have obeyed if it really had been a question of safety, but she felt fine and there was no way she was going to give up only a few hundred feet from the summit. The final ridge to the summit included two very narrow snow ridges – you could have sat astride them – with a sheer drop into nothingness and then rocks and ice, and although they were all roped together it was still a very precarious and difficult climb. The fact that Vicky doesn't like heights has never seemed to her a reason not to climb the highest mountains in the world, but getting across that second ridge on McKinley took every ounce of her nerve and courage and determination. Her goggles had cleared a little by that time and she obviously did not have altitude problems. She focused and concentrated as hard as she could and made it safely across.

So the summit was reached, but even the panoramic view of the snowy peaks and ridges all around, the magnificent weather and the fluttering prayer flags at the top couldn't lift Vicky's mood. She felt, for the first time, as if she wasn't welcome at the summit. It had been a horrible climb, and there were the two difficult ridges to negotiate again, on the way down. She was apprehensive and her confidence was low, but she managed well and the descent went very smoothly. As she came down the hill into the top camp Morris told her she was moving unbelievably well. She felt pleased, but still out of sorts: it was all very well saying that after the hard bit was over. Little did she know there was something far more difficult and terrifying waiting for her the next day.

It happened at about 16,000 feet. Just a tiny wrong moment on a narrow ledge which skirted a rocky outcrop. Vicky was edging her way round, roped in front to Morris, who was already out of sight behind the rock, and behind to Chris who had not yet come round the ledge. (Eric had gone down this section by a different route.) Vicky had all kinds of bits and pieces hanging off her pack and it was heavier than on the way up. They'd decided to make only one journey down to the foot of the headwall (instead of the two they'd made on the way up) so everyone was carrying extra. As Vicky edged around the ledge, something on her pack brushed against the rock, just a nudge, no more, but it was enough to make Vicky stick out her foot instinctively – into nothingness.

She fell only about twelve feet or so, until the rope tightened over the overhanging ledge, but below her was the void: 3,000 feet of air and sky and then rocks, cliffs and ice. Vicky looked once and then forced herself to look only upwards, to think and to work out how to get back on to the ledge. She can't remember if she shouted out to Morris or the others. She certainly heard nothing, but surely they must have felt the tremendous jerk on the rope when she fell, surely they must be standing out of sight, taking the strain? As she dangled there, completely unable to haul herself back up on the rope, her huge pack a dead weight on her back, she considered trying to take it off and let it plummet to the earth. But she realised she had so much of the kit, cookers, fuel and bits of tents that this would have serious implications for everyone. She couldn't jettison the pack. The wind was blowing as she hung there, desperately trying to think of a way to get up the rope and craning her neck to scan the ledge.

At that moment a face appeared, peering down at her.

'Hello,' said the face, in an American accent.

'Hello,' said Vicky.

'You're a gal!' said the American.

Vicky still giggles helplessly when she relives the most surreal conversation she has ever had in her life. She had no idea what was happening or who this person was.

'Yes, I am!' (After all, with all the mountaineering kit on, you can't always tell . . .)

The face above smiled broadly.

'Oh, I'm so pleased to meet another woman! I've got this terrible problem, you see. You'll understand it. I'm with all these men and they don't understand at all. I've got hammer toes and my feet are so sore.'

Vicky couldn't believe what she was hearing. She thinks, in hindsight, that this mysterious climber (whom she never saw again) might have been suffering from the altitude and didn't know what she was saying. At any rate, there was nothing Vicky could think of to say except:

'Oh, really?'

'Yes, you understand, don't you? I'm so pleased to have met you. Goodbye!'

And she was gone! Leaving Vicky hanging in space, completely bemused. She tried to swing from side to side to see if she could hoist a leg up and get a grip on the rock with her ice axe and crampons, but she was hanging too far out from the face. And then, quite suddenly, she remembered the jumar attached to her harness, the one she'd used to get up the fixed rope on the ice wall. She unclipped it and thought, without much hope, 'I'll give it a try. If I can just inch my way up the rope to a point where I can get purchase with my crampons, maybe I can haul myself over the ledge.' To this day she doesn't know how she managed it, against gravity and geometry, pulled backwards by 50lb on her back. How did she get over the lip of the ledge? How on earth did she manage to get to a standing position on the ledge, without knocking against the rock and falling again? She has no idea, and very little memory of doing it.

What she does remember, very clearly, is that when she got round the ledge to Morris, he started pulling on her rope and shouting to her to hurry up. She remembers cursing and swearing at him, but can't remember if it was out loud or not. She has a vague memory of Chris shouting something from behind her – maybe, 'Are you all right?' – but she couldn't turn round because Morris was setting a cracking pace. Down they went, descending the headwall at 14,000 feet and stopping for some food. And nobody mentioned what had happened. Nobody said a thing. Maybe, Vicky wonders now, they were afraid she'd burst into tears like she had on the ice wall and they thought the best thing was to say nothing. In hindsight, she thinks perhaps they were right. If anyone had shown her sympathy she might well have become emotional. Or maybe they all just wanted to get down quickly. Vicky still doesn't know.

It might have been the adrenalin of the fall, or the relief of being on the way down, but Vicky had tremendous strength and energy on the descent. They kept going at the foot of the ice wall, picked up their sledges, trekked back down the Kahiltna Glacier, and up Heartbreak Hill to Base Camp. Vicky steamed up the Hill with the rest of them and immediately started digging platforms and putting up tents. That evening they dug up the

8

THE DARK MOUNTAIN
CARSTENSZ PYRAMID

When we climbed over the fence our vehicles were waiting to take us back through the mine, away from the mountain. But other men with guns were also standing by the jeeps. Frankie went forward to speak to them and we could see that urgent discussions were taking place. He turned away, circled behind me and hissed in my ear, 'Vicky, you very sick. Altitude. You sick.'

I looked at him. 'Pardon?'

'You have a problem. Altitude. You must be sick.' He was hissing even louder, and casting worried glances at the men with the guns.

I realised that something had gone wrong, and we were all in danger again. Apparently the only way we were going to get out of this situation was for me to pretend to be ill. Feeling awkward, I slumped to the ground, holding my head and groaning, and rocking backwards and forwards. The rest of the team looked at me in astonishment. They had no idea what was going on.

At this point, one of the men fired his gun.

In the seven years which Vicky spent climbing the Seven Summits, on only one trip was she so badly scared that she feared for her life. This was not like the adrenalin-charged battle through the blizzard in Antarctica, or the shock of falling off the ledge on Mount McKinley, or even the serious struggle for survival in the hostile conditions on Everest. On the expedition to Carstensz Pyramid (also known as Puncak Jaya) in Papua, Indonesia, she found herself more than once in a situation where her life was in imminent physical danger – but not from the mountain: it was the journey to and from the mountain which proved so perilous, by a route which was forbidden and which could have ended in disaster. This was the hill Vicky had been apprehensive about all along, but her concern before she went was that she knew it to be the most technically demanding of the Seven Summits, involving the ascent of what is basically a 3,000-foot mass of rock. The climb did turn out to be a challenge but she could never have imagined the dangers she would face before she ever set foot on the mountain and after she had successfully summited it.

Actually, the ascent of Carstensz could be said to have taken nine months in total because Vicky attempted it twice: once in November 2000 when the group had to turn back before they got within fifty miles of the mountain, and then the return trip in August 2001. From beginning to end, the attempt to climb the sixth of the Seven Summits was frustrated and prolonged by a mixture of political unrest in the region, heavy Indonesian bureaucracy, changes of plan and itinerary, horrible weather and a little local difficulty involving armed guards and trespassing in the world's largest open-cast mine.

Vicky was all set to go in November 2000, just five months after her return from Mount McKinley. It had been a tough year, personally, professionally and in terms of her climbing. She had come back very late from the trip to Vinson, arriving in Inverness on Christmas Eve, 1999. Work at North of Scotland Water was very busy, because the Chief Executive was leaving and Vicky was involved in the process of finding a new one. When her mother died at the end of January, Vicky had to be away from the office for a week or so, and for the next few months after her return, she was fully stretched at work. At the same time, outside the office, she was battering away at her punishing training regime for Mount McKinley, grieving for her mother and trying to deal with the process of buying the cottage at Balquhidder, which was causing strain and tension among the three sisters. She went to Alaska to climb McKinley, came back to work and immediately began to plan for Carstensz.

She chose to go with Jagged Globe, the company which had organised the expedition to Vinson Massif. It would be far too costly, complicated and time-consuming to organise a trip to Carstensz on one's own because the mountain is remote and the region is politically unstable. Carstensz Pyramid is named after the Dutch navigator, Jan Carstensz, who claimed he saw snow-capped mountains only 4° South of the equator when he was sailing across the south-east Pacific in 1623. He had indeed seen the mountains of the Sudirman Range, which rises in the western central highlands of Papua, the Indonesian half of the island of New Guinea. At 16,024 feet (4,884 metres), Carstensz is the highest peak in the range and the highest mountain in Australasia.

Papua and its neighbouring province of West Papua were called Irian Jaya until 2002, when the Indonesian government granted increased autonomy and agreed to the name changes. This followed many decades of unrest after the Dutch pulled out of what was then called Netherlands New Guinea, in 1961. The eastern half of the island was a territory of Australia and has been the independent state of Papua New Guinea since 1975. Two years after the Dutch left, Indonesia annexed the territory, which is rich in gold and copper reserves, and re-named it Irian Jaya. Since then there has been a growing movement for secession from Indonesia. The Free Papua Movement (OPM) wants a referendum for independence and rejected the autonomy measures offered by Indonesia. Many of the 2.4 million Papuans feel that, at best, they are neglected by Jakarta and, at worst, they have been exploited by Indonesia's control over their gold, copper, timber and land. Most Papuans live below the poverty line, despite the fact that the province has enormous mineral and forestry reserves. This is a vast territory of heavy jungle, mangrove swamps, broad rivers, equatorial mountains and remote valleys; it has numerous tribes and more than 250 languages. There are deep divisions between the many different groups in the country, but although there may not be one strong movement for independence, there is widespread resentment of Jakarta's repressive rule. The province is heavily militarised with Indonesian troops and in 1998 at least eleven people were killed and more than fifty injured when soldiers opened fire on a group of protesters.

This was the region Vicky had chosen as her 'holiday' destination. She was happy to leave all the organising to Jagged Globe, who set up the trip through an agency in Jakarta called Adventure Indonesia, and she concentrated on keeping up her fitness and putting in some rock-climbing practice. Many years before she had done an afternoon of rock climbing with Outward Bound, but that was the extent of her experience. So one afternoon in the summer her good friend Ron Swanson took her to a beach near Forres and for hours they climbed up and abseiled down the 100-foot cliffs. Ron's wife, Sue, their son, Jamie, and his wife and children came along and sat on the beach having a picnic, waving to Vicky as she sweated her way up the rock, being belayed by Ron who was safely anchored at the top of the cliff. It seemed very steep to Vicky, and it was just as well she had no illusions about her rock-climbing prowess because, suddenly, Jamie appeared beside her, unroped and smiling. 'I'll see you at the top!' he said merrily, and shot past her, moving like a quick spider. Ah, well. The point of the afternoon was not for Vicky to climb fast; it was to practise rope work, and to become more proficient at abseiling. On Carstensz she knew the key would be to keep strong and steady throughout the ten to twelve hours it would take to climb and descend the rock face.

Everything seemed to be in place for the trip until a few

weeks before she was due to leave. Activists in Papua took to the streets and declared the region independent from Indonesia. Around 2,500 delegates at a conference in the capital, Jayapura, called on the world to recognise Papua as a sovereign state. There was uncertainty about how Indonesia would respond, and it looked as if the situation might become too dangerous for the trip to go ahead. Up until the last moment Vicky was not sure whether she was going or not, but eventually she did find herself on a flight to Amsterdam where she met the guide from Jagged Globe, Robin Beadle. They flew to Singapore and met David Newman, a research and design technologist with Rolls-Royce in Derby, who had long wanted to visit Papua because of its remoteness and the tribal culture which still flourishes in the jungle villages. David was not what he calls 'a Seven Summits bagger' but he started hillwalking in his twenties and had climbed in South America and Alaska. He had brought along a video camera to film the trip and subsequently made a short documentary account of the climb, *The Carstensz Pyramid*, which won several amateur awards and was shown at the Dundee Mountain Film Festival in 2003. The fourth member of the team was John Prosser, a retired bank manager and amateur climber from Hertfordshire, who met them at Jakarta airport, along with Mr Nova, the agent for Adventure Indonesia. The plan had been to fly straight to Jayapura but instead (for reasons Vicky never discovered) they flew to the island of Biak, close to the north coast of Papua, and from there by light aircraft to the coastal town of Nabire.

Most expeditions to Carstensz today charter a helicopter from Nabire or the hill town of Wamena, direct to the foot of the hill. Vicky's team planned to fly from Nabire into the interior, to a highland village called Ilaga, and from there trek fifty miles through the jungle to the mountain. They met the final members of the team, Bob and Steven, two Indonesian guides from the island of Sulawesi, and after a couple of days hanging around in Nabire while Bob made the arrangements, it was time at last to fly to Ilaga. They drove, in the broiling heat, to the tiny airport in Nabire where their luggage – and they – were weighed, before being loaded on to a rather battered and rusty-looking Twin Otter. As well as all their climbing kit they were carrying a generator, a gift for the local governor of Ilaga which they hoped would smooth their journey to Carstensz.

The pilot smoked all the way as they droned over mile after mile of rain forest. The island has one of the richest arrays of flora and fauna in Indonesia: over 600 species of birds, including cassowaries, parrots and birds of paradise; 150 species of lizards, myriad species of beetles and spiders and an impressive array of poisonous snakes; thousands of different types of orchids also abound. There are crocodiles, anteaters, butterflies, tree kangaroos and wallabies all to be found on this, the second largest island in the world. As they flew further and further into the highlands, Vicky and the others were looking down on thickly jungled areas where many tribes people had had no contact with the outside world until very recently.

Stubbing out his last cigarette, the pilot nonchalantly brought the plane in to land on a rough clearing. Half the village had turned out to watch and as soon as the plane taxied to a standstill a group of men arrived to unload the cargo and luggage and carry it the half mile or so to the village. These were Dani people, members of one of the most populous tribes who live in the central highlands, predominantly in the Baliem Valley. The first man on to the plane was wearing nothing but a penis gourd, the traditional dress which is gradually dying out as these ancient communities have increasing contact with tourists and travellers from the outside world. Ilaga was a memorable mixture of the old and the new: traditional round Dani huts with pointed grass roofs, and very basic wooden houses being built on the outskirts of the village; men in penis gourds, and others in western T-shirts and shorts; small black pigs, the Dani's most prized possession, trotted around the village, not far from the wooden mosque and a wooden shed which turned out to be the bank. At first Vicky felt rather awkward, as if she were intruding into a way of life which would inevitably be affected, for good and ill, by outsiders, but everyone was so friendly and open that she soon relaxed.

> We stayed in a traditional hut and in the mornings the children came and sang outside to try and get us to come out and play with them. They were great fun. There was a big cleared area where they had a volleyball net and we played volleyball in the evening; some of the mothers were fantastic – they played with a baby tucked under their arms! And one day we strung a rope between two trees and practised a Tyrolean traverse – pulling yourself by hands and legs along as you dangle upside underneath, your feet hooked over the rope. Practically the whole village turned out to watch us!

They were only supposed to stay there for a day or so before starting the fifty-mile trek through the jungle to Carstensz, led by some of the men. But it soon became clear that something was wrong: the departure kept being put off, and Bob, the Indonesian guide, was distinctly nervous about any of the team going off on their own to explore. He would come after them and steer them back to the main village. Then one morning, Bob suddenly announced that they had to leave. They could not go to Carstensz because the men were not available and the governor of the village wanted them to leave. There was a change of atmosphere that morning at the market place, a tension which was unmistakable, but all that Vicky and the others could glean was that there was some trouble brewing, either with another tribe or with armed men near the village. Bob had radioed for a plane to come and collect everyone, and as soon as it arrived they were bundled quickly onboard. After promises from Bob that he could get them to Carstensz by a different route, they were flown straight back to Nabire. Everything was shrouded in the vagueness of language difficulties, and the uncertainty of being in a country where none of them really understood the cultural and political complexities. It turned out, according to David Newman's documentary film, that there was a threat of terrorist activity by local Papuan independence supporters and the Ilaga people quite naturally wanted the Westerners out of the way.

Whatever was behind the Ilaga affair, it was the end of Vicky's attempt to climb Carstensz. When they got back to Nabire, they made dozens of calls to Mr Nova in Jakarta, and to Jagged Globe, but no one could arrange another route into Carstensz. Eventually, when it was clear that the trip was off and the only alternative was to fly home again or stay on in Indonesia and have a holiday and after much toing and froing and negotiating, Mr Nova put together a special tour for Vicky, John and David (Robin flew back to the UK). The three of them spent a wonderful fortnight exploring Sumatra and the surrounding islands, finishing with a boat trip to see the Komodo dragons. It had been a frustrating trip, but Vicky was undaunted; as soon as it was clear the trip to Carstensz was not going to happen, she had made her mind up to return the following year; with only two summits left to do – and Everest the dream at the end of it all – there was no way she was going to give up.

*   *   *   *   *

Nine months later, in the dusk of Thursday, 9 August 2001, Vicky was sitting in a Toyota Land Cruiser, her hood pulled over her head. Beside her were John Prosser, David Newman and two other members of the team, and in the front passenger seat Frankie, one of the guides, was giving instructions to their driver. The rest of the team were in the car behind. In a few minutes they would begin their clandestine journey to Carstensz Pyramid. This time, instead of approaching the mountain from the north, through the jungle, they had flown to the south coast of the island, to the mining town of Timika. The plan was to drive from Timika up into the mountains and, under cover of darkness, steal through the Freeport-McMoran copper mine, along a gravel road which runs for miles through this massive mine, and climbs 10,000 feet up into the mountains. That was the plan, but it was a risky one.

The US-based mining corporation, Freeport-McMoran Copper and Gold Inc., has been mining in the area for nearly forty years under an exclusive licence from the Indonesian government signed in 1967, which was extended for another thirty years in 1991. The Grasberg Mine (also known as Freeport Mine) is the world's largest open-cast mine, containing the largest single gold reserve and the second-largest copper reserve of any mine in the world. It sprawls for ninety square miles across the scarred remains of what was once a 13,450-foot mountain. Its revenues are enormous and in 1995 the company paid over $1 billion to the Indonesian government in taxes. In the past, the mine authorities used to give permission to climbing parties to use their road, but in the 1990s environmental groups became increasingly vociferous about the amount of pollution generated by the thousands of tons of waste material dumped every day into the Aghawagon River, and human rights organisations highlighted allegations of violence against local protesters by the mine's security forces. Faced with all the negative publicity, the mine closed its gates to travellers in 2001. They allowed vehicles to carry climbers' luggage through the mine, but expected the climbers themselves to get to the mountain by alternative routes.

This was the forbidden road which Vicky and the others were preparing to travel. Not only was it closed to tourists, but no women at all were allowed in the mine. It had not been the original plan when they had booked the trip. They had been assured that Adventure Indonesia would organise a trip in a military helicopter which would fly them from Timika to the base of Carstensz but, as had been the case the previous year, plans changed and the agent said that the helicopter ride would not happen after all. Instead, their Indonesian guides, Bob, Frankie and Steven, said that the military would provide vehicles to transport them to the mine entrance where they would then transfer to other vehicles, acquired and driven by 'friends' in the mine who would take them through the mine checkpoints, all the way to the mountain, no questions asked.

The Indonesian military in Papua were there to quell any civil unrest and local opposition activity. Although it was never said in so many words, the team knew that, by handing over the correct amount of money to the right people, the vehicles would be arranged. The same went for the mysterious 'friends' in the mine. David Newman says that throughout that second trip, he felt they were never given the full story of what was planned and how things were to be arranged; the climbers were being sheltered – and to some extent, excluded – from the way of doing business there. They had put a great deal of pressure on the agent to arrange alternative transport when the helicopter plan failed, and this was the solution he had come up with. Vicky and the others knew that going through the mine was trespassing, but they were never clear just how illegal the enterprise was: was it so illegal that it was dangerous, or was it just daring? All they knew was that it would have to be done carefully and secretly. Vicky found it rather unnerving.

> The atmosphere in Timika was very tense. We were told we had to be terribly careful and mustn't talk about where we were going to anyone. We weren't to mention anything about going through the mine, or even going up the mountain. We – and all our huge amounts of kit! – were just supposed to be there for a nice holiday. Frankie assembled us all in the hotel

room in Timika one evening for the final briefing, and locked the door. He told us we weren't to talk loudly or get cross or raise our voices in case someone outside the room heard us. David filmed all this secretly under the table, I'll never know how. Frankie told us we were going to be smuggled through the mine, through the night, in some vehicles which they had managed to 'acquire' from mine staff, presumably by the handing over of money. This is how we were to get through the checkpoints, with all of us hidden out of sight.

Vicky wasn't scared, but she was nervous. The whole thing seemed highly serious, and at the same time rather ridiculous. There were eight climbers in all to be smuggled through: Vicky, John and David; an American called Scott who was guiding another American, Lawrence; two Australians called Ralph and Geoff, one a lawyer and the other a banker; and a Japanese businessman called Kenji. The expedition had not been organised by Jagged Globe because Vicky, John and David were unhappy at not being reimbursed for the previous year's abortive trip; instead, they had contacted their agent, Mr Nova in Jakarta, and asked Adventure Indonesia to set everything up. He had brought together what was, in effect, a group of individuals who wanted to climb Carstensz, but he had not organised it as a trip with a qualified guide, because Vicky, David and John wanted to keep the costs down. The American, Scott, was only there to guide *his* client, and Frankie, Bob and Steven were just local lads who did a bit of climbing. For this, the most technical of the Seven Summits, Vicky was, for the first time, going to climb without an experienced guide leading the team.

So it was with a mixture of trepidation and excitement that they all squeezed into the two Land Cruisers that night, on the first stage of the journey. There was a third vehicle which carried their luggage and seems to have travelled through later.

Each car had a driver and an army guard. (Only later, at Base Camp, did Vicky discover that the guards had been carrying rifles, when one of them gave the Japanese business man some target practice one morning.)

As they approached the first checkpoint they all crouched down below the seats and the cars passed through without incident. They drove for many miles through more checkpoints up to a purpose-built complex in Tembagapura, a town in the middle of the mountains. There were many large buildings, three or four storeys high, built out from the edge of the hillside which housed, according to their driver, some 4,000 miners. It looked more like a work camp than a town. This was where the first change of vehicles took place, after everyone had been bundled into one of the flats, which consisted of a room with a couple of beds, a toilet and a kettle. They were given some food and told to keep quiet and wait. After what seemed an age, they were chivvied out again to where a big minibus was waiting, the type used for ferrying mine workers to the site. The driver was a mine employee, and everyone was now travelling in the same vehicle. And so the long drive through the mine proper began. David Newman could hardly believe the scale of the place. Their minibus would pass by massive dumper trucks, carrying tons of rock and ore, whose wheels towered above the bus. Each checkpoint was a nerve-racking few minutes for Vicky and the other passengers squashed down on the floor.

> I stopped breathing each time. I couldn't see anything, just the flash of searchlights roaming over the car. I could hear calling and shouting in the dark, but we had no idea what was going on. The whole trip took hours and hours. We were driven up about 10,000 feet so you can imagine how huge the distance was – and it's all open-cast mine. It's absolutely mammoth. I remember that after one checkpoint we were driven through a labyrinth of underground tunnels, probably where they had

blasted through to get to the other side of a shoulder, or to get to higher ground. I had never been in tunnels like that before. By this stage we were in a small truck and the roof of the tunnel was just a little higher than the truck so it was very claustrophobic. It was rough-cut rock, turning and twisting for miles. There were some signs at some intersections, lengths of wood attached to the rock with names painted on them, very roughly.

They made it safely through the last checkpoint after they left the tunnels, and then began to climb steeply up a wet, sludgy dirt track. They were on the home straight now. Suddenly, in the distance behind them, they heard the faint wail of sirens and, craning her neck, Vicky could see searchlights dancing about on the road below them. The alarm had been raised.

Frankie twisted round in his seat to peer out of the back of the minibus and shouted that there were five security cars chasing them up the hill. He yelled at the driver to put his foot down and the truck bumped and clattered its way up the steep track which was littered with rocks and slurry from the mine. In the back, Vicky and the others were bounced around like peas in a tin and, as she glanced behind her, she could see the headlights of the pursuing cars getting closer and closer. When their truck suddenly screeched to a halt beside a fence, Frankie screamed at them all to grab their rucksacks and get out. 'Climb the fence,' he shouted. 'Get over the fence. Run up hill.' There was utter and absolute confusion.

Frankie was really scared, but I can't remember exactly what happened. I just remember being petrified. Remember it's pitch black and we had no idea where we were going. When Frankie shouted at us to get over the fence, I had no idea why. I suppose it must have been the perimeter of the mine and he wanted us to get over before the cars caught us, but they were only yards behind us, lights blazing and sirens howling. We scrambled up and over the fence and Frankie was shouting at us to run, but it was utterly dark and we didn't know where we were going. There was a rough track and he screamed at us to keep running. Just think about it: we'd been driven up to 10,000 feet, and the track was very steep, a rough, rocky path and we had to run up it, in the darkness, terrified.

Even now, several years on, when she has had time to relive the events and try and work out what happened, Vicky is still very unclear about that night. It had a nightmarish quality about it: she was being chased, but she didn't really know why, or who was pursuing her, or where everyone else was. She knew beforehand that they were not supposed to be driving through the mine, but what was the worst that could have happened to them? Surely they weren't being chased by people who seriously wanted to harm them? They were only trespassing on a mine, for goodness sake! But in that panicked flight up the hill, with Frankie's shouts and the wail of sirens ringing in their ears, rational thought was not uppermost.

It was mayhem. I heard gunshots when I was running up the track. Were they shooting at us, was it warning shots? I don't know now. I can't describe what it was like, trying to get up that track. Searchlights were dancing all around us, and Frankie yelled at us to turn our head torches off. We had to run up 100 feet or more, at 10,000 feet, when we'd been sitting in a truck for hours. Our lungs were burning and hearts bursting, and when we stopped someone threw up and others were coughing up blood. And most frightening of all, Frankie was beside himself with fear, and that made me very afraid.

In all likelihood, Frankie had a lot more to fear than the climbers. He was Indonesian, he had (presumably) bribed a lot of people to smuggle them through the mine, and these people would be at risk of losing their jobs, or worse. No wonder he was scared. It seems, since everyone got through safely, including the Indonesians and the two guards, that either the pursuit was *not* life-threatening or more money exchanged hands. Both are probably true, although when there were guns involved and people were firing them in the darkness, Vicky could be forgiven for thinking they could all have been seriously harmed. It had all been such a sudden shock. They had been told by Frankie back at Timika that the enterprise was risky, but they had had no idea of how risky. They had been told that if they behaved and followed orders, the chances are they would get safely through to the mountain. And so it had turned out, until those last panicked moments at the very end.

All these reflections came later. At the time, Vicky and the others had only one thought in mind – to get away from danger. They eventually stumbled on to a small plateau and tried to get their breath back. The path climbed again and, as soon as they were able, they started off again. No one was chasing them. The sirens and the flashlights had stopped. Everybody seemed to be accounted for, although Vicky is not very clear on this point either. All she knows is that by the time they arrived, almost dead on their feet, at their planned first camp at the foot of a cliff called Zebra Wall, everyone seemed to be there but the tents were not. They all sat down, in some misery, on their rucksacks, on an area of rough hummocky grass pitted with pools of water. It had started raining in the night and continued to rain for most of the trip. They may have been near the equator, but the mountain rose up from the equatorial rain forest and the prevailing weather conditions for the trip were warm and humid, with mist, long periods of rain and, as they climbed higher, snow.

The tents arrived some time later in the day, carried by porters from the road head where the vehicle arranged by

Frankie had delivered them, and everyone tried to settle down and acclimatise. They were at about 12,000 feet, and many people were in a bad way because of the sudden ascent the night before. Everyone was suffering from headaches and Vicky soon developed a cold as well. Zebra Wall was a dreary place to be for the next two days. The weather was grey and foul, the water running constantly down the rocks flooded the tents, the landscape was rocky and bleak, and a heavy curtain of grey mist hung over everything.

As part of their acclimatisation they trekked to where they would set up Base Camp, in a valley near the base of Carstensz. Over the next ridge they could see the mountain, a massive slab of grey rock, flecked with snow. It looked very high and serious, especially through the binoculars. Vicky didn't much like what she saw.

It looked very steep and a long way up! There were fixed ropes on the route we were to climb, which had been there for some time, put there by previous teams. I knew we would be climbing in the dark, very early in the morning, so which ropes do you choose when you're in the dark? When ropes are left lying on rock faces the wind rubs them against the jagged rock edges and, in time, cuts through the rope casing. If you get through the casing, there's no strength in the rope and it will snap when weight is put on it. Looking up at these ropes, we didn't know how strong they were. It was potentially going to make the climb very dangerous.

They trudged back to Zebra Wall in the mist and drizzle for a last night before the move proper to Base Camp. Carstensz Pyramid was now firmly in their sights.

* * * * *

Sunday 12 August
Up at 6.30 a.m., breakfast at 7 a.m. Felt bad – sick, headache and general malaise. I need to drink more. Packed everything up to take to Base Camp. Carried tent, sleeping bag and thermarest. Took approx. two hours and weather was good! No rain until about an hour after we arrived. If weather is OK, plan is to do Carstensz at 3 a.m. tomorrow.

It was no surprise to anyone that the weather was not OK the next morning. During the night it began to sleet and snow and when Vicky got up at 2.10 a.m. it was still rainy and snowy, with a strong wind. They drank tea for breakfast and Frankie decided that the weather was too bad to attempt the summit that day. So they all went back to bed. Vicky's diary entries for that day illustrate the tedium and frustrations when a group of strangers are at the mercy of the weather and forced to hang around with each other for hours, waiting to climb:

Went back to tent after Frankie called off summit, but ended up trying to sort out tent, mop up the water and then went back to bed. Frankie said we could try again at 5.30 a.m. if there was a weather window, but weather too bad so went to sleep again till 8.30 a.m. Fried egg breakfast. John cross that we didn't at least agree to set off and see how weather behaved. John, David, Kenji and I went for a walk over to the bottom of the fixed ropes on Carstensz. Back to Base Camp in the rain – everything is so wet! I am feeling lousy with a bad cold/flu which started today. John and I played Scrabble with the Aussies in my tent – we won! Bed at 10 p.m.

There was, however, one bright spot in that day of waiting around in the damp of Base Camp. While Vicky and John were playing Scrabble in the tent with the Australians they heard voices outside. Vicky's name was called, and when she went

out, one of the guides told her that there were some people
looking for her. To her huge delight, it turned out to be two
women from the Ilaga village she had stayed in the previous
year. They were on their way somewhere (she never found out
where), and had stopped at the camp and chatted with the
guides. When they heard that Vicky was among the climbers,
they asked to see her and when she came out of the tent they
threw their arms around her. It was almost incredible: up there,
in the shadow of Carstensz Pyramid, two women from a tiny
village fifty miles away had happened to pass by on that day,
and remembered Vicky from the year before. 'That almost
made the trip for me,' says Vicky. 'It was a lovely moment.' Later
that night she wrote again in her diary:

> Will try for summit again at 2.30 a.m. tomorrow. Cold now
> very bad, and shivering a lot. Hope I will manage!

*   *   *   *   *

They got away this time. After hot chocolate and salty boiled
noodles for breakfast, they set off in the darkness, head torches
and helmets on (in case of falling rocks), and walked in single
file over the pass, down into the valley and up to the foot of the
mountain and the start of the rock face, the North Wall. Getting
started was quite hard for the first few feet because it was steep.
Vicky took a deep breath, clipped on to one of the fixed ropes
and had a fair old scramble to get up on to the rock face proper.
Then they were climbing, slowly, slowly for hours, up rough
white limestone, heading for the West Ridge which leads to the
summit. Vicky can't remember the dawn coming up. She was
concentrating so hard on clipping and unclipping on to ropes,
scrambling, climbing and, in sections, jumaring up the rock face,
i.e. pulling herself up on a fixed rope by a mechanical device
which can be slid up the rope, but which locks when you put

your weight on it. As she had feared, some of the fixed ropes were in poor condition, so she tried to climb without putting weight on the rope: there was nothing else she could do.

After four pitches of climbing and some free scrambling, they came to a steep snow slope which they would have to traverse. Bob put up a fixed rope for them to clip on to and they moved slowly across, one by one. The two Americans were nowhere to be seen. They had gone off earlier than the rest because Scott, the guide, knew that the main group would be very slow. They wanted to get ahead so that when it came to the most difficult bits of the ridge, they would not be stuck behind the rest of the group. If Vicky had experienced a secret relief when she knew Scott was in the team, because that meant an experienced climber would be with them after all on Carstensz, it was no longer the case. They were on their own up there.

After several hours they reached the summit ridge. From there they could gaze across mountains, valleys and glaciers and, at nearly 16,000 feet, they were breathing heavily with the effort of climbing. They could also see the scarred and gouged expanse of the Grasberg Mine below and hear, even at this height, the distant roar of the mine machinery. The ridge was about six feet wide, falling steeply away to either side, and covered in loose rocks and snow. They moved slowly, unroped, which was rather dangerous, considering their exposed position and the terrain underfoot. The most technically difficult part of the ridge was a wide gap – rather like a missing tooth – which they had to get across by abseiling down thirty or forty feet, climbing up and over a huge rock, and then jumaring up eighty feet on the other side of the gap. The climb on the other side was made much more difficult by a big overhang which meant that the fixed rope was hanging away from the rock face.

There were one or two much smaller gaps to come, further along the ridge, but this was the major one and no one was looking forward to it.

We all stopped and huddled and got our slings and ropes and descenders ready on our harnesses. It was all quite daunting, looking down into the gap. I felt very exposed because just past the edge of the gap there was a 3,000-foot drop. And I could see that, going up the other side, under the overhang, I would be swinging on a rope, at 16,000 feet, in mid-air. It looked very hard.

It took them hours to get across. One by one, they abseiled down and clambered, scrambled and jumared up over the huge rock, then climbed up out of the gap. Six climbers plus the three Indonesians, Bob, Frankie and Steven. One of the Australians, Ralph, had great difficulty in getting up over the overhang on the other side because his jumar got stuck. Stephen had to climb up behind him to help. When Vicky's turn eventually came she, too, had problems on the climb out. It is difficult to describe the strength and effort required to climb up a rope which is dangling at 16,000 feet in mid-air and you are having to pull your own body weight every inch of the way. You are attached to the main rope by a jumar which is clipped on to your harness. Your feet are sitting in small loops of rope wrapped round the main rope – a prussic loop. There is an almost balletic rhythm you have to find in order to move up the rope: one hand moves the jumar up the rope while you bring your knee up to your waist, steady yourself, push down on the prussic loop and heave yourself up the rope, first one foot, then the other. It is seriously strenuous work. Add to that the fact that the main rope will be swaying in the wind, you will be wobbling and stopping for rests, and, at this altitude, your lungs will be burning. When Vicky eventually reached the overhang she simply got stuck; she did not have the strength to move her jumar up over the lip of rock and pull herself over. In the end, Steven leaned over the edge and pulled her up bodily.

By the time everyone got across and they continued up the

ridge, they had been climbing for nearly twelve hours. The weather had turned again and it was raining steadily. The mist had descended and by the time they reached the summit, all Vicky wanted to do was turn around straight away. There was little elation at having reached the top. She knew that they would all be tired on the way down and getting across the big gap was likely to take even longer. They stopped long enough on the summit to sign the sheet of paper in a little canister which had been left there for climbers, and then they turned to face the long descent.

It all got rather messy and dangerous on the way back. The weather was turning colder and it was getting late, and when they got to the big gap Kenji and David were exhausted. Then there was an accident. Vicky was standing below Kenji, on the climb up out of the gap, when suddenly he fell off the rope. Vicky tried to break his fall, but he landed very heavily on his back. He had forgotten to clip his jumar on to his harness, so there had been nothing holding him on to the fixed rope. In fact, this was Kenji's very first experience of rock climbing. He had also never abseiled before, and here he was on Carstensz, a complete novice, struggling up and down rock faces in the dusk, 16,000 feet up. He was dazed but physically fine, and he sat for a while to recover while Vicky climbed up. The others were still abseiling down the other side of the gap and it was another half hour before everyone (apart from the two Australians who had gone on ahead) was safely back on to the ridge. By this time it was almost dark and from that point on they were descending by the light of their head torches. David, Kenji and Frankie were so tired their heads were bowed as they walked.

Down the ridge they went and down on to the rock face. They were clipping on and off ropes, abseiling time after time, and trying to find the next set of fixed ropes by the light of their torches. Then Vicky got cold feet. Not literally, but at the sight of one of the abseils which involved going over an edge of rock and then swinging in underneath the overhang. It was dark and cold and she simply couldn't bring herself to clip on to the rope, edge backwards to the lip of the rock, lean back and jump outwards and backwards so that she would drop down the rope a little; if you don't do it that way, you swing back in too soon and either smash your face against the rock or hit your head. Vicky was tired and she simply could not summon up the energy and courage: she froze.

The others had all got down, but everyone was exhausted. Below her, Vicky could just make out the figure of Bob, so tired that he was falling asleep against a rock. John called up to her to take her time. He knew how frightened she was and tried to talk her down, gently and calmly. It took a long time, but eventually she got down – to find that everyone else apart from John had already gone. They had gone on ahead, leaving John and Vicky to find their own way down the mountain.

It was no use. They couldn't find the next fixed rope. For what seemed like hours, Vicky and John scrabbled around in the dark, trying to find their way to the rope, keenly aware that one step too far in the wrong direction could be a step into the void. What on earth were they to do? At that point John turned to Vicky:

'Hang on, Vicky. I know what we'll do. Let's climb back up to where these nice people were in that cave. They'll help us.'

I looked at him in astonishment. 'What do you mean, John?'

'You know, these nice people who were smiling at us when we were passing the cave. Let's go back up and ask them the way.'

I realised that John was so exhausted and dehydrated that he was hallucinating. There was no way we could on. So we found a ledge and stayed there for the night. We roped ourselves up to a big rock, wrapped up in our big, silver insulating space blankets and hunkered down for the night.

It was a cold, uncomfortable night. At one point Vicky looked far across and down into the valley and could see the head torch lights of the others bobbing up and down as they made their way up over the pass, back to Base Camp. At least somebody would be sleeping in a tent that night. The hours passed somehow, but in the morning all was transformed. The dawn revealed that they were sitting in a recess, on an edge, not far from where the rock face fell away steeply. But instead of feeling afraid or exhausted, Vicky was curiously elated. In the still of the dawn, gazing across the valley to the hills beyond, she felt like an eagle in her eyrie, thousands of feet above the rest of the world, alive and free. Free as a bird.

She and John made their way down the remainder of the rock face, and set off for Base Camp. On the way they met the Americans, Scott and Lawrence, who had come looking for them, bringing hot tea and sweets. When they saw Bob he explained that everyone had been so exhausted the night before that he had no choice but to get them off the hill as quickly as possible. There was no point in arguing about it now.

Everyone just wanted to get back home. Vicky was pleased to have climbed Carstensz, finally, after more than nine months, but it had been one of the least enjoyable climbs she had done. It had been dank, miserable and scary and the landscape of bare rock, unrelieved by anything green, had been made even bleaker by the incessant rain and mist. They rested for several hours at Base Camp, ate a wonderful lunch cooked by Bob and then packed up their stuff for the walk back to Zebra Wall. They were due back at the entrance to the mine around dawn, so they sat around for the rest of the day, playing Scrabble and chatting.

They set off before dawn, as usual in the pouring rain, down the track to where six days before they had fled in terror. An hour or so later they emerged at the road head and sat down to wait for their transport. They saw a mine vehicle with a blue flashing light on top coming up the track. Once again it looked as if something had gone wrong: instead of being met by the minibus Frankie and Bob had arranged, they were faced with a car with two security guards carrying guns. Frankie went up to the first car and started talking fast and earnestly to the guards. Then he walked behind Vicky and whispered urgently to her to pretend that she had altitude sickness. She was surprised and confused, because she had no idea what was going on, but the tension in Frankie's manner and voice was unmistakable. He urged her again, hissing in her ear, so she slumped to the ground, startling the guards so much that one of them fired his rifle into the air above her head. She groaned loudly and bent her head, muttering to John under her breath to come and pretend to help her. John half-heartedly patted her on the back, still not sure what was going on. Then Scott realised what was happening, rushed over to her, telling her in a loud voice that she would be fine. Frankie turned to the group and translated what he had been saying to the mine guards: he had been telling them that they were waiting at the road head because they needed to get Vicky to the medical centre at the mine. But Vicky had no intention of being separated from the rest of the group.

There was more shouting and gesticulating between Frankie and the guards before everything suddenly changed again.

'Get up. You OK now,' Frankie called to Vicky.

The two security guards got back into their car, turned round and headed back down the track. Everyone was stunned. What on earth had all that been about? According to a breathless Frankie, the guards were harmless and had actually come to pick up their luggage, as had been the arrangement on the way in. The problem seemed to be that the car had come too early, before the porters had brought the luggage down to the road side. The vehicle which *should* have been there was the minibus to take them all back through the mine – and that was the vehicle that Frankie did not want the security guards to know about. He had managed to persuade them to go away again and return for the luggage in a couple of hours. Meantime, the group trudged back up the road for a little and waited in the rain until the minibus finally arrived.

When it eventually turned up, everyone piled in. They drove at breakneck speed back down the mine road, through the tunnels and checkpoints, being stopped by no one and finally arriving back at Timika about ten o'clock in the morning. One moment stands out in Vicky's memory on that furious drive back. When they were coming through the tunnels. John turned to her and whispered, 'What are all these people doing in the tunnel? They're all smiling at me.' He was hallucinating again, and Vicky replied, 'Don't be so daft, John. There's nothing there.' The next moment, she saw them, too. Gnome-like faces on the sides of the tunnel walls, happy and grinning. They were obviously suggested by the shapes of the rock and the headlights glinting over them, but it gave Vicky a shock. She had no idea she, too, was at that point of physical exhaustion and emotional tension where she was beginning to see things that weren't there.

That was their last day on Papua. They were supposed to stay another night in Timika, but Frankie said they needed to leave straight away. He had changed their flights. So after a bite to eat and the briefest of washes at the hotel, they were bundled once more into the mine cars and driven straight to the airport and ushered on to a flight to Jakarta. Everyone was agitated and tired and disturbed by the speed of events. Whatever machinations had been going on behind their backs about the route through the mine, they never learned the full truth. It was enough that they had got out unscathed. And Vicky, leaning back in her seat on the plane to Jakarta, already had her eyes fixed on a point far beyond the rigours and scares of the past week, far beyond the flight home, far beyond the return to work. There it was, the magnificent prize at the end of the journey – Everest.

9

THE ROAD TO EVEREST

It was a glorious early spring day in April 2002 and Vicky was cleaning her house in Aviemore. Her job at North of Scotland Water had come to an end and she had already packed up all her belongings and transported them down to the cottage at Balquhidder. Today was the day for cleaning the house from top to bottom before she left for good. All the doors and windows were open, the wind was blowing sweetly from an egg-blue sky and Vicky was down on her hands and knees in the kitchen, Marigolds on, scrubbing the floor.

She heard a voice calling from the living room.

'Hello. Is anyone at home?'

She scrambled to her feet just as a strong-looking man with a pleasant face popped his head round the door and said, 'I'm Sandy Allan.'

This was the internationally experienced Scottish mountaineer and guide whom a friend had recommended to Vicky as someone who could get her ready for Everest and climb with her. For the next half hour they talked about her plans but Vicky, typically, found the whole thing faintly embarrassing; just as she had squirmed during the phone conversation all those years ago with Jon Tinker when he asked her about what climbing experience she had for Elbrus, so this sudden meeting in her kitchen among the mops and brushes felt surreal and slightly ridiculous.

I remember giggling partly because I'd been caught washing the floor and partly because it seemed such a ridiculous conversation. 'I want to go up Everest!' It was as if I'd asked him, 'Can you tell me how to get to Sauchiehall Street!' It just didn't feel serious on that sunny day in the middle of the kitchen, with me in my Marigolds, to be talking about getting to the top of Everest.

Embarrassing or not, she did ask if he would guide her and Sandy agreed to take her on. However, he wanted to test her first and see what she was capable of, so he said she would need to do some high ice and rock climbing in the Alps and, equally importantly, try an 8,000-metre (26,250-feet) peak as training for altitude and endurance. She would have a year to get ready for Everest.

It was six months since Vicky had returned from the dramatic climb of Carstensz. When she got back to the office, she expected to settle straight back into her usual routine of fitting in training, hillwalking and expedition-planning for the next summit around the demands of her job. Little did she know that in six months she and most of the senior management at North of Scotland Water would be made redundant. The rumours of big changes to come had been rippling around the corridors since the early months of 2001, and by late summer there were lapping more strongly: it looked as if the Scottish Executive was going to re-organise water services yet again. When Vicky first joined North of Scotland Water in 1996, it had been one of three new regional bodies created to take over water provision from the local councils and authorities; East of Scotland Water and West of Scotland Water were the other two organisations. Now it looked as if these three bodies were going to be scrapped and a new, single authority created, and by the end of the year it was confirmed: there would be one Scottish water authority, to be called Scottish Water. It was clear, therefore, that major job losses among the most senior people in North, East and West would follow: Scottish Water would need only one chief executive, and there were currently three; only one HR director would be needed, one finance director, one operations director, and so on. Unless she successfully applied for the post of HR director with the new company, Vicky would be out of a job.

The atmosphere in the head office of North of Scotland Water in Inverness was extremely tense. Now it was the turn of people at Vicky's level to face the sort of re-organisation and change which they had been negotiating and pushing through with the unions for the past five years. Over that period, new working practices, salary structures and working conditions had been introduced, and the work force had been reduced from about 1,900 to 1,200. What Vicky and the other directors had achieved at NOSWA had been applauded by the Scottish Executive, but it would not save them from the radical overhaul to come.

Vicky was, of course, concerned about her future, especially as she was about to spend an enormous amount of money on going to Everest, but she felt that she perhaps did not have as much to lose as some of the others; she had no ties or responsibilities, so she knew she could afford to lose her job for a few months until she found something else. As the date for the interviews drew closer, Vicky contacted a company in Aberdeen which specialised in coaching people for new careers, and asked them to come and work separately with the directors. They would discuss options for the future, work on CVs, and advise on career plans. When her own turn came, Vicky sat down in her office with the consultant, Jane Owen, and they began to talk. Jane asked her first if she was going to apply for the job of HR director for Scottish Water.

'Yes,' said Vicky.

'Do you want it?' was the next question.

'Oh, yes, definitely.' But as they talked, and explored the job and what Vicky had been doing up until then, something happened. To Vicky's astonishment Jane looked at her and said,

'You don't really want this job, do you? I'm not feeling that you're totally committed.'

When Vicky heard the question, it was as if she had just been waiting for the opportunity to say,

'You're right. I don't want it.'

The job did not feel right and she was applying for it, not for herself, but out of responsibility towards her team. If she got the job in the new company, they would feel more secure about their own futures. Jane began to dig deeper. It is a conversation which has lived with Vicky:

Jane said, 'OK, then, what do you want to do? Forget the fact that you feel you've got to apply: what do you really want to do?'

I gave her some stupid waffle about new challenges and other jobs, but she persisted.

'Come on, Vicky,' she said, 'you're not being honest. What is it you really want to do?'

I said, rather irritably, 'OK then, I'll tell you what it is – I want to climb Mount Everest.'

And she just looked at me, and said,

'Then you must do it.'

And tears welled up in her eyes! And that started me off. Jane, who was supposed to help us with our futures and boost our confidence and make us feel confident – she had us both reduced to tears. She was so perceptive that I think she realised the great significance of our conversation and it touched us both deeply.

It was a moment of revelation for Vicky. She had been planning to climb Everest ever since she embarked on the Seven Summits, and was determined to do it, but it had always been a dream, something far-off which caught her imagination, and was still out of reach. In all those years of climbing she had shared her dream with very few people, and certainly with hardly anyone at work, but here she was positively declaring it:

I can't really describe what happened inside me. I can't describe how I was feeling. It wasn't elation, it wasn't fear. I felt light, as if a huge weight had been lifted. It was almost as if what emerged at the surface was the truth. You can make a lot of noise and run along madly in life, and then, gently, the truth of who you are and what you want comes up to the surface, calmly and quietly. And there was the path.

Vicky *did* apply for the job even though she did not want it and was not surprised when she was not appointed. With her redundancy package and her savings, she was ready to direct all her energies and resources towards getting to the top of Everest. She made contact with Henry Todd, a man well known in Everest circles, who lives in Kingussie when he's not at Base Camp; he had been running expeditions to the Himalayas since 1989 and was among the first people to open up the highest peaks in the world to the non-professional climber. ICE 8000 started as Himalayan Guides and its stated aim was to give 'mountaineers from outside the exclusive groups of international mountaineers' the chance to participate in high-altitude expeditioning. The company did this very simply: by organising the trip from start to finish, getting all the permits, planning the travel, hiring the Sherpas, organising the equipment and accommodation, finding guides, and taking responsibility for all the logistical and bureaucratic requirements.

It's very expensive to climb Everest, and when Vicky found out just how much it was going to cost, the prospect of being without work for months was less appealing, so, never one to do things by halves, she immediately set up her own company. She had no idea how to go about it, so she asked her lawyer

he welcome party on arrival at Illaga in Papua, Indonesia

Two very different cultures happily
working together to unload the luggage
from the plane at Illaga

Vicky marching with the children
in Illaga on her way to practise
rope work in the nearby trees

Market day in Illaga – you could feel the tension due to the unrest in the area

Part of the largest opencast mine in the world seen from the start of Carstensz Pyramid

Snow near the equator! – part way up the
3000ft rock face on Carstensz Pyramid

Looking across the gap, or 'slot', to the 50
overhang on the summit ridge – the mos
difficult part of the climb

n the walk-in to Base Camp – view from
ngboche looking up to Everest in the far
stance and Ama Dablam on right

Vicky's home for two months at Base Camp

axing at Base Camp – John Wylie watching
:d Atkins trying out a prototype for a new
oxygen system he was developing

Porter carrying a full load in to Base Camp

Puja taking place at Everest Base Camp with the Khumbu Icefall in the background

Patrick at Camp 2 with Lhotse in the background

Vicky at the top of the Icefall with Pumori in the background

The team (left to right: Vicky, Ian, Kevin and Rob) trying on oxygen masks for the first time Base Camp – a relaxing experience!

Avalanche near Base Camp

Vicky crossing a ladder at the top of the Icefall

Horizontal ladder in the Icefall

Vertical ladder in the Icefall

Looking down at the Lhotse Face from Camp 3 to Camp 2 and Western Cwm

Looking back down the Lhotse Face from Geneva Spur with the tents at Camp 3 below the Yellow Band

From the South Col looking up at the summit 3000ft above

Gasping for breath on the summit ridge, with the Hillary Step in view

Vicky on the summit of Everest

Some of the team relaxing at Base Camp after the big climb. Left to right: Chris Warner, Sue and Henry Todd, Bob Jen, Clive Jones, John Wylie and Vicky

The 'Welcome Home' sign Tommy MacGregor made for Vicky's return to the glen after she'd completed the Seven Summits in 2004

Receiving her honorary doctorate from Magnus Magnusson at Glasgow Caledonian University in 2005

what she should do first. The lawyer put her in touch with an accountant and, after one meeting, and less than a month after she had left North of Scotland Water, Vicky had set herself up as Vicky Jack HR Consultancy and was ready for business. The first offer of work followed very quickly, and in May 2002 she carried out work for Network Rail in Glasgow. Once again she was back in her routine of working and training, only this time it wasn't going to be enough to canter up and down Munros with sixteen telephone directories on her back. For Everest, a different sort of training was required.

*　*　*　*　*

'Where are you climbing tomorrow, then?' asked a big, brawny man.

It was August and Vicky was sitting at a long trestle table in the Torino Hut, a mountain hut on the Mont Blanc massif in the Alps. The hut was full of people, eating and talking and relaxing at the end of the day's climbing, exchanging information on routes and chatting about tomorrow's plans. Everyone mixes in and shares the tables, and Vicky had got into conversation with a group of very fit-looking French climbers.

'Oh, I'm going to do the Tour Ronde,' she replied airily. She was feeling happy and relaxed, having spent the last few days doing some climbing on a rock face just south of Chamonix, and then on a mixture of snow and rock on the Cosmique Arête, not far from the hut. The man stared at her. Vicky is slight and doesn't look like a climber, and the man was clearly surprised.

'Are you an experienced climber?' he asked.

'No, not really.'

'How much have you done?'

'Oh, I've done about three climbs since we got here at the beginning of the week.'

Vicky has always underplayed her abilities and experiences

when talking to 'serious' mountaineers; she considers herself a high hillwalker, not a mountaineer. The man opposite her obviously took her at her word because he looked aghast and asked, 'Who are you climbing with?' When she mentioned Sandy Allan's name – a well-known name in the Alps – the worrying reply was, 'Does he know what he's doing?'

Sandy knew exactly what he was doing. When he started rock climbing with Vicky, first in Scotland and then in the Alps, he had realised that she was very, very fit and, as he described her, 'quick and very competent on her feet'. She had been extremely good on the Cosmique Arête – 'she had a natural ability on snow and ice-climbing', is his opinion – and he was confident that she would cope well with the North Face of the Tour Ronde.

The conversation with the French climber, however, hardly filled Vicky with confidence for the next day's climb. As she recalls, 'it fairly put the wind up me.' Up to this point she had been quite happy with her progress. She is, in fact, an experienced and capable climber who is far more than a hillwalker. Jon Tinker, the world-class mountaineer who led the expedition up Elbrus, describes Vicky as 'very strong, and a good climber. She's someone who has worked really hard to become a good climber and she's no burden to anyone on the hills.' The training which Sandy Allan was putting her through was to get her used to what he called 'airyness'; that is, he wanted her to climb high on steep, exposed ascents on ice and rock and snow, where she would be using the front points of her crampons and two ice axes to climb vertically. He was teaching her how to climb technically, and not just to scramble. Vicky had been doing well, but the conversation that night in the hut left her wondering just exactly what Sandy had in store for her the next day.

She soon found out. The Torino Hut is about three-quarters of an hour's walk from the north side of the Tour Ronde. They left the hut before dawn, having fought their way through the mass of climbers in the porch area pulling on boots and crampons and heaving on their rucksacks. Ice climbers leave early because it is best to climb the north faces when they are frozen solid. Once the sun comes out and the temperature rises, all the boulders which are cemented into the rock walls and ice faces are loosened and, as Sandy describes it, 'the face becomes a bowling alley. Any climbers still on the face in the bright alpine sunshine or below areas of the mountain which are exposed to the sun become proverbial skittles for the rocks.'

Vicky's head was heavy and sore from the altitude, her pack was heavy and she felt slow and cumbersome as they trudged away from the hut. It was still dark when they reached the foot of the snow face and Vicky saw the obstacle she would need to overcome – a huge bergschrund. A bergschrund – from the German meaning 'mountain crack' – is formed when a glacier breaks away from the rock face and leaves a huge gap below and usually a massive overhang, above which the glacier continues. There were a lot of climbers already in front of Vicky and Sandy and by the time their turn came, the bergschrund was fairly mangled and churned up. In the cold darkness, her head heavy and her limbs barely warmed through, Vicky was struggling.

I found it hugely difficult. Sandy is a good climber so the bergschrund wasn't a problem for him, but I made heavy weather of it. Sandy kept shouting down to me, 'Come on, come on!' and people behind us were beginning to get agitated. I had to jump up the gap, and climb out and then up and over the slight overhang, with gravity and my own body weight pulling me backwards. And it was all in the dark!

It took her a long time, but eventually she made it and got herself up on to the long, steep climb. And from then on she loved every minute. She had passed the test, and Sandy was obviously satisfied with her competence because, from that point on, they climbed together. Vicky was roped to him, but he was not attached to anything; if he had been less sure of her ability, he would have been fixing ice screws in to the ice face and tying on to them. Instead, Vicky climbed behind him, keeping the rope at the correct tension, with not too much slack. If she *had* slipped, Sandy would have driven his ice axes into the snow and that would have held them. They climbed steadily, Sandy making steps for Vicky by kicking into the ice and snow with his front points, and Vicky stepping into them. Many times she would be leaning into the face, her front points dug into the ice, and her heels hanging in mid air. It was exhausting, frightening and exhilarating.

Vicky does not like heights. That is, to say the least, an inconvenience for someone who set herself to climb the highest mountains on the seven continents and, you would think, a particular disadvantage for Everest. But she looks on it as just another hurdle to get over, another problem to tackle. Sandy knew that Vicky would need to feel confident and competent for certain sections of the Everest climb; the Lhotse Face, for example, a 3,700-foot wall of glacial blue ice which rises at 40-degree and 50-degree pitches, with the occasional 80-degree angle. He was pushing Vicky just hard enough to make her fit and strong and capable for the mountain, and she, for her part, knew that the key was to keep pushing upwards, steadily and carefully.

When we were climbing together on these steep faces I just had to concentrate on going up. Don't be distracted by looking down. And then, of course, you occasionally have to look down and you think, 'Oh, no, this is not good. I don't like this.' But then you pull yourself together and you keep going. You have to be so aware of what you're doing, so sharp-minded, and do it neatly, smoothly and, hopefully, swiftly. There is a tremendous amount of concentration required, so that is what you focus on – not on how it feels to be so high.

Sandy was encouraged by Vicky's climbing in the Alps. The next test would be to do an 8,000-metre peak in the Himalayas. The two easiest – i.e. non-technical – ones were Cho Oyu in Tibet, the sixth highest mountain in the world, and Shishapangma, also in Tibet, the lowest of the fourteen 8,000-metre peaks. Sandy had climbed Cho Oyu several times so they decided to go for Shishapangma. Vicky finished her contract with Network Rail at the end of August and they went off on the month-long expedition. Vicky didn't particularly enjoy it, though. The weather was poor, and the climb itself was just sheer hard work. The aim was to push her stamina and her ability to cope at altitude, not to improve her technical climbing, and from that point of view it was a hard test. She was sick at top camp, from a combination of altitude and food, but they did not climb much above 23,000 feet because on summit day the weather closed in, there was heavy snow and a risk of avalanches, so they turned back.

By this time it was October 2002, and Vicky was planning to leave for Everest in March 2003. As the months wore on, her life became busier and busier. Network Rail asked her to work with them again until Christmas, she was going up hills at the weekends and, from January to March, she embarked on the final phase of her training. Sandy put her in touch with another climber, Alan Dennis, a Canadian who divided his time between Aviemore and Canada, spending each winter working for the Scottish Avalanche Information Service in Aviemore. The SAIS publishes daily forecasts of the avalanche, snow and climbing conditions at five climbing areas of Scotland during the season – Glencoe, Lochaber, Creag Meagaidh, and the Northern and Southern Cairngorms. Alan was based at the Scottish National Outdoor Training Centre at Glenmore Lodge and his job was to go up into the Cairngorms every day, assess the conditions and write a report which was then posted on the SAIS website for climbers to consult. The website is the main source of information on snow and avalanche conditions and on a busy winter's day it can receive 3,000 visits.

Vicky went out with Alan two or three times a week as his assistant. They would vary their routes up over Cairngorm and in and around the corries. At a particular point on a snow face or slope Alan would do a snow profile. He had years of experience and knew where to sample the snow. He would cut a pit and remove a side of snow so that he could examine the cross-section of snow and read the different layers. Vicky's job was to note down all the measurements as Alan called them out. It sounded like good secretarial training, but what made it useful training for Everest?

Learning about avalanches and types of snow was interesting, but not critical. What was critical was that I was out on the hill for hours on end, three days a week. It got me fitter and stronger. We were walking and climbing with heavy packs, and occasionally we climbed routes in the corries after Alan had finished work. I was out on the hill in all weathers: high winds, blizzards, white-outs, and it was pretty scary sometimes. It was good training because it got me used to being in bad weather, battling for hours through discomfort and cold and adverse conditions. We would climb up steep snow slopes, stop halfway, dig a platform in the snow and tie ourselves on. Then Alan would dig a pit there. I was using every moment to try and get as ready as I could for Everest. I really benefited from lots of walking on snow with crampons, being on a ledge in nasty conditions and tying on, and starting to use two ice axes. I wasn't going to need two ice axes on Everest, so I was going beyond what was needed and, by doing that, I was getting more comfortable with what lay ahead.

Vicky knew just enough about what she would face on Everest – or, rather, she knew as much as she wanted to. Where some people might get hold of lots of books on the subject, pore over maps and surf the internet for information from the countless Everest websites, Vicky was content to find out just enough to help her get to the top. She talked to Henry Todd and from him she had a pen portrait of the climb, by the South-East Ridge Route, which would involve negotiating the Khumbu Icefall and going across crevasses on ladders; a long steady plod up the glacial valley of the Western Cwm to the foot of the Lhotse Face; then a long, hard, steep climb up the Lhotse Face to Camp 3 where Sherpas will not stay because the avalanche risk is so high, but where everyone else does because they are not strong enough to keep going straight on to Camp 4; after that it's a hard climb to Camp 4 on the south col, very tiring because you are now on oxygen; and finally, the arduous summit day, first up a broad couloir, or gully, then along the south-east ridge, up the Hillary Step and then on to the summit. Vicky talked to other climbers and had a broad idea of what to expect, but that was all. She did not read other people's accounts of climbing Everest; she did not go over the route, inch by inch, finding out about all the different obstacles she would encounter. She simply did not want that kind of information.

I did have some books, but I just couldn't bring myself to do that sort of research. It wasn't fear – well, maybe it was, deep down – but I felt: No, I'm not going to look at these books today. And then tomorrow never came. It is funny, I know. Other people pore over maps and routes and want to work out exactly where they're going. I didn't want to know because, if you see too many hurdles in front of you, you're going to be demoralised and give up before you start. I didn't want to know about all the hurdles. I knew that, whatever they were, they were going to be huge.

One of the things she was most apprehensive about was crossing the crevasses in the Khumbu Icefall. She knew that the Sherpas laid ladders across them, sometimes four, five or six ladders lashed together length-wise, secured at either end, and climbers had to walk across the rungs of the ladders, in big boots with crampons, keeping their balance. Henry Todd's advice to her was very practical: 'Just go and practise it, Vicky. Buy a couple of aluminium ladders from B&Q – that's the kind they use in Everest – and have a go in the garden.' So that is exactly what she did. She got the ladders, laid them on the grass and tried to walk across on crampons.

> I felt very wobbly. I thought, 'This isn't good.' Then I put the ladders on the shallow steps at the back of the house so that they were at an angle, because Henry had told me they weren't all horizontal in the Icefall and this would test me going uphill and downhill. I tried that, and fell off. So I got walking poles and I could do it fine with them, but you can't use walking poles when you're going across a crevasse. And I was beginning to think, 'Oops, I'm not going to manage this.' Eventually I gave up and thought, 'Well, it can't be that bad or nobody would be able to do it on Everest. I'll just take it as it comes.'

Vicky's philosophy of life is that everything can be accomplished in 'bite-sized chunks'. She did not want to go to Everest with the undiluted enormity of the task weighing her down before she had taken a step on the mountain. So she disciplined herself to absorb only what she needed for the immediate task-in-hand. She reduced the vastness of the mountain to what she knew best: climbing Munros. So each 3,000 feet she climbed would be a Munro, and then another, and another until summit day – another Munro. That was how she prepared mentally for the highest mountain in the world.

Other people were rather more worried. Some of her friends,

quite naturally, were concerned about the dangers on Everest. Over 3,551 people have reached the summit since Sir Edmund Hillary and Tenzing Norgay in 1953, but the success rate is low: only about one in nine people who get to Base Camp reaches the summit. And the death rate is high: more than 211 people have lost their lives on the mountain – in 1996 alone, fifteen people died – and many of these bodies are still up there, frozen and abandoned because it is too difficult at these heights to bring them down. Bad weather, avalanches, falling down crevasses, altitude sickness, exhaustion, accidents – the list of risks and dangers on Everest is long, and the reaction of some of Vicky's friends was to draw their breath in sharply and say, 'Are you sure you know what you're doing?' Her friend Shona was nervous for Vicky, but congratulated her for having the ambition and enthusiasm to try. Vicky remembers that Jean, another climbing friend, was a little more doubtful and concerned. It was hard for Vicky because, although she appreciated her friends' concern for her, she had made the decision, had come to terms with the risks and had a very positive attitude herself.

> I didn't want anyone to be at all negative and say things like, 'Have you thought that you might not come back?' It was OK for me to say that, but I didn't want anyone else to say it. So, aside from the fact that I was working really hard up until Christmas and then training hard and was very busy, I really didn't want to see any of these friends because I was afraid their concern would hold me back.

Jean noticed that Vicky drew away slightly from her friends during that period.

> She started training much, much harder, leading up to Everest. And she almost – she didn't cut herself off from her friends, but she wasn't really there; she was just wanting to go, she was

so single-minded, she just seemed to have one track in her mind and anything could have happened to anybody and she would hardly have noticed. And I don't mean that in a bad way. It was almost as if she'd focused everything on going up Everest.

This was the only way Vicky knew to prepare herself as well as she could for the mammoth task in front of her. She had to be well trained, focused, organised and committed. There *were* times when she wondered if she would come back, but these were intellectual musings rather than fearful imaginings. She has a powerful ability to shut off negative thoughts and look forward with a quiet confidence. When a decision is made, it's made and all her energies go into achieving what she has set herself to do. She duly went to her lawyer and prepared her will, and then she threw herself into the final weeks of preparation. As well as climbing with Alan, she was cycling, running and lifting weights for upper-body strength.

The practical organisation of the trip took huge amounts of time and patience. She gradually made lists of clothes, equipment, books, food and other essentials to pack, and the floor of her living room began to disappear under mounds and mounds of kit. She still has the lists, written on A4 lined paper, with lines crossed out, things added, little notes to remind herself of items she still had to get. They are delightful and vivid snatches of the past. One list, entitled simply 'Food', illustrates her anxiety about keeping herself strong and well nourished in an environment where most people lose a great deal of weight because at altitude the appetite goes and the body has great difficulty in digesting food. The list includes the following:

Peppermint tea
Complan sachets
Nuts
Raisins

Cremola Foam
Good chocolate – Green & Black
Marmite
Oat cakes
Multi-vitamin pills
Oil capsules
Vitamin C effervescent tablets
Dried fruit, e.g. apricots

Cremola Foam was the little tin of flavoured powder which turned into a fizzy drink when mixed with water and Vicky always used to take it up Munros with her. It was a favourite treat for children in the 1950s and '60s and the original owners of the company lived in her home town of Kilmacolm but, by the time Vicky was going up Everest and was looking for tins to take with her, Cremola Foam was no more – Nestlé stopped production in 1998.

Her clothing lists have dozens and dozens of items and include everything from crampons, gaiters, several different types of gloves, sleeping bags, disposable camera, penknife and climbing boots to shampoo, toothpaste, a sewing kit, spare bootlaces, Elastoplast, string, ibuprofen, toilet roll, fruit pastilles, sunscreen factor 50 and small poly bags. And all around the edges of the list are little one-word reminders to herself: passport, credit cards, address list, flight info. Another list – 'Everest prep.' – begins with five notes:

Doctor appt. – antibiotics
Diamox (for altitude)
Check vaccinations
Haircut
Waxing

Vicky cannot for the life of her remember now why she was planning to get her legs waxed for climbing Mount Everest or

whether she ever did. That is what makes these lists so fasci-
nating: they are so ordinary and down to earth. Going to
Everest was a curious mixture of the realisation of a dream
which was the pinnacle of the previous six years' climbing, and
of the everyday planning and tedious organisation of the thousand things she needed to do to get ready. Anyone who finds
it hard to pack for two weeks' holiday in the sun can imagine
the nightmare of packing everything you need for nearly three
months in the Himalayas, living in tents and climbing the highest
mountain in the world.

There is one other list among Vicky's papers which is
completely different from the rest. This is her sponsorship list.
She decided that she would try to offset some of the cost of
the trip by raising money from companies and individuals.
Her 'Possible sponsors for Everest in May 2003' list includes
the Royal Bank of Scotland, Kwik Fit, Scottish Water,
VisitScotland, Tiso (the mountaineering shop) and Baxters.
She also noted down various media contacts for publicity,
because she knew that interviews on television and radio and
in the press would generate interest and help with sponsorship. She *did* receive a lot of media attention, particularly in
the newspapers, who were delighted with the story of a middle-
aged woman who would be the oldest British woman to summit
Everest and the first Scotswoman to complete the Seven
Summits; but her attempts to find sponsorship were, by her
own admission, pathetic. She only managed to raise about
£3,300 which included – as yet another list faithfully records
– a tax rebate of £146.89 from the Inland Revenue! Vicky laughs
at how much she hated asking for money: 'I can't ask for things
for myself. I can ask for things for other people, not for myself.'
Which is another way of saying that she is a successful
businesswoman when it comes to work and being effective in
a specific role, but that when it's personal – as personal as
asking for money to realise her dream – well, that's something

quite different. And Everest *was* intensely personal; this was her path.

*   *   *   *   *

It was Monday, 17 March 2003. The day was sunny, the sky blue, the first snowdrops were nestling in the grass at the back door, and it was time to leave. Everything was packed, all the last-minute phone calls had been made. Vicky did a quick scan round the cottage and stood at the back door for a moment, looking across to Beinn an t-Sidhein and down to the River Balvaig, glittering in the sun. She locked up the house and nipped across the single-track road to say goodbye to her neighbours, Tommy and Betty. They assured her that they would keep an eye on things while she was away, and Betty reminded her once again of a little-known historic link between Balquhidder and the first ascent of Everest. When Betty was a girl, her parents ran the village Post Office and one day in late summer 1953 she saw two men walking along the road, one tall and fair-haired and the other shorter and dark-skinned. It was Edmund Hillary and Tenzing Norgay, come to Balquhidder to visit Edwin Kerr, a local man and accomplished climber, who had been an important sponsor of the 1953 expedition. Everyone in the village knew Edwin Kerr and his connection to the Everest ascent, which had been national news for weeks, and Betty was thrilled when Tenzing Norgay came into the Post Office and spoke to her parents. Fifty years later, Vicky was renewing that link between the glen and Mount Everest.

Vicky had been thinking a lot about her mother these past few weeks, and imagining what Maureen would have said about it all. She knew absolutely in her heart that her mother would have said, 'Go and do it, Vicky', and that gave her great strength and comfort. She knew how proud her mother would have been of her, and that meant more to her than anything else. She waved to Tommy and Betty and drove down the road. The journey had begun.

10

THE HIGHEST MOUNTAIN
IN THE WORLD
MOUNT EVEREST

Wednesday, 26 March 2003, Namche Bazaar
Sat and watched everyone in the main room of the lodge
where we're staying. Porters were huddled around the wood
stove which had a huge kettle on it. Television was blaring,
mostly on CNN – Day 7 of Iraq War, not good. Sitting opposite me was an English father and daughter with a map working
out a route. Then they played a strange card game. An English
guy called Tommy who is climbing Everest sat across from me
– he ate an omelette with about 10 boiled potatoes. Also a
Japanese girl and her Sherpa – she was furious because her kit
had not arrived. I had a yak steak for supper and went to bed
at about 9.10 p.m.

Namche Bazaar is a village in the Khumbu region of Nepal. It
clings precariously to the side of a beautifully terraced hill more
than 11,000 feet above sea level, and is the gateway to the high
Himalayas. This bustling, lively place was stop number two on
the walk-in to Everest Base Camp for Vicky and the other
members of the team. They had flown from Kathmandu to
Lukla, a small town huddled in a steep-sided valley so narrow
that the plane lands on an airstrip which slopes uphill. Porters
collected all the heavy luggage and, after an overnight in the
village of Toktok, the group started on their trek in towards

Base Camp. There were five of them: Henry Todd, who ran Himalayan Guides and had organised the trip, and with him his girlfriend, Sue, who was coming as far as Base Camp; Vicky's climbing team mates were Ian, a QC from Edinburgh, and Kevin, a nurse from Tennessee. The sixth member of the party, Rob, a trainee medic from Bristol, would join them later at Base Camp.

The streets of Namche were thronged with climbers, porters and tourists, and Vicky was in her element, relishing the excitement of being here – on her way to Everest at last, fifty years after the first ascent by Sir Edmund Hillary and Tenzing Norgay in 1953, and in the year of her fiftieth birthday. She climbed up through the streets, from one level to the next, puffing and panting in the thin air, standing aside to let yaks through, and stepping over the scrawny-necked chickens which were skittering about. Women in long scruffy skirts and old, torn down jackets were sitting out on doorsteps, knitting and crocheting the Nepalese hats with the distinctive dangling ear flaps which were on sale in the little gift shops. Up above the village, before the clouds came down, Vicky caught her first distant sight of the topmost tip of Everest, one tiny white crest amongst a heaving sea of colossal mountains which stretched endlessly to the horizon.

Everest is a massive three-sided pyramid which straddles Nepal and Tibet. Its South-West Face is in Nepal and the North and East sides in Tibet. Over the decades since 1953, the mountain has been successfully climbed by several different routes from both sides of the border. Hillary's route from the Nepal side was the one Vicky would take – by the South Col/South-East Ridge, an extremely long climb over four main sections: through the perilous Khumbu Icefall, up the vast, seemingly unending valley called the Western Cwm, to the steep and icy Lhotse Face, and then the punishing summit route from the South Col to the South-East Ridge, via the Hillary Step and finally on to the summit. This route is sometimes disparagingly called 'the yak route' by people who presumably have never climbed

The final day's trek from the village of Dughla was a hard one. They climbed up about 1,500 feet from the village and passed through a long valley, gently rising all the way, past two other villages and then eventually arrived at Base Camp after seven or eight hours. For the final two or three hours the track was narrow, littered with boulders, rocks and stones and steeply precarious on some sections, so that when yaks came lumbering in the opposite direction, having delivered their massive loads to Base Camp, it was a tight and rather perilous squeeze to get past them. The track lurched up and down, and they were forced to scramble over and around the rocks and house-sized boulders which are the detritus – the moraine – gouged out by the massive glacier which formed the Everest valley. Base Camp itself was at the foot of a steep path of scree, which wound its way down a huge mound of rocks and boulders and edged into the wide, grey glacial valley which would be Vicky's 'home' for the next two months.

Everest Base Camp sits 17,500 feet above sea level in a bleak and barren landscape. It's not an attractive campsite.

It's a huge area, covered in rocks, boulders and scree. All the rock and scree and gravel is actually on ice – we are on a glacier which is still moving – and when the sun warms it up, ice melts from around huge boulders and leaves them exposed and liable to tumble over. You set up your tent on an uneven surface of rocks and stones, and then the sun comes out, melts the ice underneath, gaps appear, rocks are dislodged, everything shifts, and you have to move your tent again. You could hear the ice shifting and creaking all the time, and then there were avalanches further up the valley; we watched them during the day, and could hear them roaring down in the middle of the night. It felt as if we were camping on a living thing.

But it was exciting and thrilling, too. It may have been uncomfortable and bleak, but Vicky felt happy and contented there.

Henry, the expedition leader, had sited their camp quite far back from the main throng, so it was quieter and less busy. Vicky could sit outside her tent, and look over to the Khumbu Icefall, about twenty minutes' walk away, and revel in the knowledge that she was really here at last, and ready to fulfil her dream of climbing Everest.

After a couple of days' rest, they were ready for their first foray into the Icefall. Henry wanted them to get their first taste of one of the most dangerous and extreme places on the long climb to Everest. The Khumbu Icefall is a war-zone of ice, a battlefield of glacial destructiveness. High above Base Camp is a vast valley called the Western Cwm, and over the millennia an ancient glacier has ground its way down through the surrounding mountains until, squeezed at the mouth of the valley, it collapses and tumbles like a waterfall in a mass of broken and ruptured ice into the next valley where Base Camp sits. Anyone climbing Everest by the South Col/South-East Ridge must first get through the Icefall.

The scale of it is frightening. Some of the ice blocks are the size of houses. The crevasses and chasms are hundreds of feet deep. And the landscape is constantly changing and shifting, as thousands of tonnes of ice continue to inch their way forward. The only way through it is via the fixed ropes and ladders which the Sherpas – the ice doctors, as they are known – put in at the beginning of the season, and maintain over the four to six weeks of the season. The ladders are tied together and slung over the black crevasses, some horizontally, some on an incline, and some lashed together vertically up the highest and most irregular of the ice blocks. It is a Brobdingnagian wilderness of ice where climbers are reduced to Lilliputian figures, scrambling over a dangerous giant who is breathing and shifting all the time, and at any moment may rear up and effortlessly snap the ropes and ladders.

This was the place Vicky had been imagining when she

gamely arranged her aluminium ladders in the back garden at Balquhidder and practised walking across them in her crampons. She wobbled off several times back then; now it was the real thing. There would be no stepping safely on to the grass if she lost her balance; now she would be picking her way on a shaking, bending ladder across an icy void. Vicky, Ian, Kevin and Henry set off in the morning carrying day packs with water, something to eat and spare jackets. They picked their way round the tents, rocks and ice and twenty minutes later they arrived at the foot of the Icefall.

Henry turned to us all and said, 'OK we'll stop here and you can put on your crampons.' That was when I realised we were at the point of no return. Now I was at the Icefall, for real! It was quite a long climb to get to the first ladder and we puffed and panted our way around narrow crevasses and across snow-bridges. Some of the chunks of ice in there were a hundred feet high, and had up to six ladders lashed together to climb up and over. We climbed over huge buildings of ice, squeezed past others, edged around great chasms, following the fixed ropes put in by the ice doctors. There were creaking and rumbling noises from the ice going on all the time. At one point Henry said we would go up and have a go at 'the macaroni', as he called it: an absolute mess of twisted, collapsed, piled-up ice blocks that looked ready to tumble at any moment. It was very scary going across my first ladder. There was about a 100-foot drop beneath it, and the ladder was anchored on either side with big metal ice stakes, and a loose rope on both sides. I clipped on to one rope and started across. My feet felt like blocks of lead as I tried to place my crampons so that the ladder rungs would sit between the spikes. And you can't dawdle: you've got to keep moving and get across quickly because there's lots of traffic, with Sherpas carrying loads and packs, and they move like greased lightning. They don't want to be – and shouldn't be – held up. I was tired at the end of it all, not just physically because I'm fighting for breath, but mentally: you have to concentrate all the time and keep a clear mind.

As the weeks pass, the Icefall becomes progressively more dangerous. The sun melts the ice, the glacier moves and ice blocks collapse and tumble. By the end of May some ladders can be swinging in mid-air because a crevasse has widened; others can be bent because a crevasse has contracted; some of the metal stakes securing the ladders are loose because the sun has melted the ice around them. The ice doctors try to maintain the route, but it is constantly changing. Vicky went through the Icefall on five return trips over the weeks, climbing a little higher up the mountain each time, returning to Base Camp to rest and climbing again to a higher camp and back down; this is the practice for climbing Everest so that you get stronger and more acclimatised each time before the final attempt on the summit. But each time she wondered whether this would be the time when something bad would happen, and she would tumble into one of those gaping crevasses. And often, as she tried to concentrate on crossing and not looking down, her eye would be drawn to the small object lying at the bottom of the crevasse, or caught on a ridge half way down: a single glove, a pair of goggles, an ice axe. In her mind the Icefall became her River Styx, an obstacle to be crossed before getting to the mountain proper.

There was also a tremendous sense of achievement, though, at getting through safely. The first time the team went all the way through the Icefall it took them almost six hours. But each time they went through, they did it slightly quicker; it never felt any easier – their lungs were still burning with the effort and mental concentration and physical stamina required were still exhausting – but they did get faster.

On Saturday, 12 April Vicky's guide, Patrick Kenny, and the last member of the party, Rob, arrived at Base Camp. Back in

February, about a month before she left for Everest, Vicky's plans to be guided by Sandy Allan had changed and Henry had put her in touch with Patrick Kenny, an American climber, guide and skier based in Utah. He had been climbing in the Himalayas since 1996 and had summited Everest in 2000. Vicky had always intended to pay the extra money for a guide on Everest because she had great respect for the mountain and wanted to make sure she had the very best chance of acquitting herself well.

> When I was arranging the trip, I was asked if I really wanted and needed a guide. And I said I did because I had never been on Everest, it was a completely different scenario from the mountains I'd done before and I didn't know how I would be on the hill. I wanted to feel safe. I didn't want to hold anyone else back, and if for any reason I had to turn back, I wouldn't want anyone else to have to turn back with me. It was expensive, but I did want that security blanket.

As it turned out, Patrick was very helpful and reassuring for the rest of the team, too. Although Vicky was his primary concern and responsibility, more often than not Ian, Kevin and Rob climbed alongside, and so they all benefited from his expertise and experience. Little did Vicky know that, in a few weeks, circumstances would change dramatically and she would end up going for the summit without Patrick.

*   *   *   *   *

The lama was a small, elderly man with a warm, delightful smile. He sat on an old mat on the rocky ground at Base Camp, chanting and praying, hour after hour, offering up respect and honour to the gods for protection on the great mountain, Sagarmatha, 'goddess of the sky'. On the other side of the mountain, the Tibetans call Everest Chomolungma, 'mother goddess of the universe'. That morning the lama was conducting the *puja*, the ceremony to bless and protect all those venturing on to the mountain; without this blessing the Sherpas would not climb.

Vicky and the others sat around a sort of Buddhist altar which had been built and adorned with candles, flags, an edible sculpture of a mountain, a prayer scarf wrapped around a stick, a brass bowl of water and lots of food and drink, including whisky and a very strong beer called *chang*. Other climbers and friends dropped in to watch for a while, and then drifted away. Vicky sat drinking tea and watching the ceremony unfold.

> The Sherpas erected a tall pole which was adorned with various flags, including the saltire, the flag from Tennessee, and the children's hospice flag, and then, radiating in three directions, streams of prayer flags which flapped and fluttered in the breeze. The belief is that the prayers will sail up to the mountain on the wind. It was a stunning sight. All our boots, crampons and ice axes were piled up and blessed by the lama. I hoped this all meant that we would be looked after on the hill.

This was not the first Everest blessing Vicky had received. On the walk-in to Base Camp the group had stopped at Buddhist monasteries where the monks had given each of them a piece of cream fabric, like a scarf, and blessed it. They also gave them string cords. The monks tied a knot in them, blew on the knot and chanted a prayer, to bring safety and the goodwill of the gods on the hill. The idea is to tie the strings round your neck and not take them off; you are supposed to leave them until they drop off of their own accord. Vicky wore her cords from the first attempt, and others from the second attempt, for well over a year; by that time they were bleached and stringy and she eventually removed them because she was going to a formal dinner and decided that grubby-looking pieces of string would not quite fit the bill as a necklace.

With all the religion and ceremony that surrounds Everest, it was not possible for Vicky to view it as a mountain like any other of the seven summits she had climbed.

It was different, but not just because of its size. There was an added dimension there. The Nepalese are religious themselves and go through ceremonies like burning juniper every time before they go up through the Icefall, and throwing sacred rice into the air, asking the gods to keep them safe. That does affect how you feel about things. I felt something beyond the normal about the mountain, but it wasn't a calm and reassuring feeling. It wasn't a feeling of inner peace – there was a draw, a power there; it was awe-inspiring.

The day after the *puja* the team made their first climb all the way through the Icefall and on up to Camp 1 at 19,750 feet. This time it took them only four and a half hours to get right through the Icefall, an improvement of more than an hour on the last time. It was a hard slog to Camp 1. Climbing out of the Icefall they were faced with more crevasses on flatter ground. The sides of the valley at this point were very steep, there was a considerable avalanche risk and Camp 1 seemed no nearer. More ladders down and up, more detours, more trudging, more panting until, eventually, they could see the camp. Patrick and Vicky were sharing a tent, and Henry and the others divided up into the other two. It was a cold, windy night with a fall of snow in the wee small hours. They were all up again at the crack of dawn and set off for Camp 2, but Vicky was feeling sluggish and tired. Her pack seemed very heavy, although she was carrying a fairly standard load of sleeping bag, carry mat, thermarest and a couple of extra bits of kit. The vast Western Cwm stretched in front of them, with the steep sides of Nuptse on the right and Pumori behind them, and Lhotse looming ahead in the distance. From the start, it was a battle:

Camp 1 to Camp 2 was awful, awful. We set off without crampons and the first thing I did was to fall and slide on my backside – not an auspicious start. The trend continued as I slid and fell several times so we stopped and put our crampons on. We had to go up and down ten huge slots – massive steep-sided trenches at the beginning – sometimes scaling ladders hanging on walls which were thirty feet high, sometimes clambering by crampons and fixed ropes up the shallower ones. And all the time, a constant, steady uphill. When the sun comes up it beats down on the Western Cwm and the heat is trapped by the high sides of the valley. It's absolutely roasting. You're peeling clothes off, but stopping to undress is the last thing you want to do when you're exhausted. Everything is an effort. It's impossible to describe how that effort and exhaustion feels. There were people away ahead of us, just tiny dots on the horizon, and we never seemed to get closer. The Western Cwm just goes on for ever. You're walking for an hour and you feel as if you haven't gone one step. There's no progress because the scale is huge and you still seem to be in the same position in relation to the mountains on either side of you. It's so demoralising.

But Vicky gritted her teeth and kept going and actually made very good time to Camp 2. In fact, by the time she got there, she felt so strong that she and Patrick, after a short rest, walked on further towards the head of the valley. There she had fantastic views – she could see the summit of Everest and the long route ahead of them: the Lhotse Face and the Yellow Band to the left, an area of sedimentary sandstone rock which was, many aeons ago, part of the seabed; and she could make out the big outcrop of rock called the Geneva Spur. It was a glorious and uplifting sight which filled her with renewed energy and eagerness after the punishing climb from Camp 1. They stayed only a short time, gazing up at the amphitheatre of hills around and above them, before heading straight back down to Base Camp.

This is the pattern for climbing Everest. You go a little higher each time, coming back down again to rest in between and making each climb longer than the one before. At these altitudes, you never feel comfortable, never feel easy, but your body does acclimatise and become stronger as it is gradually pushed beyond the limit of each new climb. Vicky learnt very quickly that it was as important to have mental stamina and discipline, as physical strength.

Everything's distorted because the scale is enormous. You concentrate on just the few feet ahead of you, and you mustn't think far ahead. Occasionally something makes your mind race and, boy, you've got to pull it back. Because if you think, 'Oh, how far is it?' you'll just get discouraged. Maybe you've been up to Camp 2 before, and this time you're going straight through from Base Camp without a break at Camp 1; if, at that stage, I'd thought, 'Oh, no, I've still got to go through that awful long trek through the Western Cwm' – I couldn't have done it. You have to discipline your mind. You curtail it and pull it right back to thinking about the immediate task, the present.

That seems the intriguing tension about climbing Everest. Vicky was in this unique place on Earth, and yet, rather than letting her mind loose to become part of that vast natural entity, what she had to do was to rein it in all the time and make everything small enough to be manageable. That was how she kept herself focused on keeping going, but it did not mean that she shut out the grand beauty of Everest:

Oh, there was such an energy, too. Like setting off through the Icefall, at night, with a big moon, and the sun starts to come up but the moon's still visible in the sky because it's so clear. And some of the nights at Base Camp, with all the stars studded around the sky, it just bowled me over. Sometimes I felt moved to tears with happiness, but if I'd started I wouldn't have stopped.

*   *   *   *   *

There is a page in Vicky's Everest diary which is covered with a rough sketch of her kitchen. One of the many things she had been trying to organise during the months of preparation for Everest was the renovation and re-design of the cottage. In the many idle hours at Base Camp she began to plan a possible kitchen lay-out. It's a wonderfully down-to-earth moment among the pages of notes on towering peaks and dangerous Icefalls and lung-bursting climbs through snow and rock. The helpful little comments underneath the drawing – 'welsh dresser: cupboards on top (glass storage), with drawers (cutlery) and cupboards underneath (plates etc)' – speak of ordinariness and home. Climbing Everest may be one of the greatest challenges someone can set themselves, but the weeks there are not one unbroken series of dramatic encounters with the mountain; much of the time, at Base Camp certainly, is spent dozing, or sitting about in tents, reading and listening to music; or perched on wobbly chairs outside the tent, chatting, or eating; or doing washing in the sun; or complaining about communications and the weather. Just like home, in fact. Except that at Everest Base Camp everyone is there for the same purpose, living in a completely unnatural environment, breathing half as much oxygen as they need to function properly, and pushing themselves to their physical and mental limits.

Still, Vicky loved Base Camp. She loved the camaraderie of being in a team, she loved her own tent with everything arranged as she liked it, she loved the purpose and the excitement of being there. But there were times when tempers frayed, when people's annoying habits got on each other's nerves, when the underlying competitiveness of a couple of hundred climbers all wanting to get to the top of the same mountain became a little wearying. As the weeks passed and the weather windows in May drew nearer, the tension in the camp grew and almost every day, it seemed, Henry would be involved in discussions with some of the men about whether the preparation was going well, why this was being done and not that. But there were the laughs, too. Like the day they all tried on their oxygen masks and sat in a row on their plastic chairs outside the mess tent, posing for the camera. And going to the Internet Café was always fun; a couple of enterprising Sherpas had rigged up some laptops powered by ranks of solar panels lying on the rocks outside the tent. Vicky sent emails to friends about how she was getting on, checked her website where she wrote occasional reports on her climb, received news from home and caught up on all the latest gossip and stories from around Base Camp. People would play cards there, chat for hours, relax and generally laze around. After the rigours of the Icefall and the Western Cwm, it was a welcome relief.

On Friday 18 April the team set off once again from Base Camp. The plan was to go straight up through the Icefall, past Camp 1 and on to Camp 2. They would rest and acclimatise there for a few days and then climb to Camp 3. Patrick pushed Vicky hard going through the Icefall and they moved so fast that they left the others far behind and overtook a team of Irish climbers, a group of Frenchmen and a party of Koreans. Vicky was very tired when they emerged at the top, but they kept on, pushing past Camp 1 and plodding on towards Camp 2. There are lovely flashes in Vicky's diary of that steely competitive edge which lurks just below the mild surface of the only woman in a company of lively, confident men:

> Rob caught up and overtook us, so I told Patrick to go ahead when we were past the ladders and on the long haul to Camp 2. I kept plodding very slowly in the heat and before I knew it, I had caught up with Rob again (aged twenty-seven and very

fit) who went quickly but stopped often for rests – the tortoise and the hare! Got to Camp 2 exhausted.

Exhausted or not, everyone had to get to work levelling the rocky, icy ground for pitching camp and that meant a couple of hours of using pick axes and shovels, lifting huge stones and cutting away at the ice. At altitude, shovelling just a couple of spadefuls left Vicky and the others wheezing and panting, and afterwards she collapsed into the tent she and Patrick were sharing. In the morning they all ate in the kitchen tent where one cook and one cook boy worked hard all day preparing full meals on just two kerosene burners, and then they sat on a great big stone slab covered with mats. This was a day for rest and recuperation, but it's never comfortable at that altitude and in that environment. Vicky was feeling quite breathless and it was an effort to eat and drink. She also had headaches and was munching painkillers. In the distance she could see the shining face of Lhotse – sheer, hard ice rising more than 3,000 feet up the mountainside. That was the next huge obstacle to overcome, the climb that had been in Vicky's mind throughout the days she had spent with Alan, in all weathers, on sheer faces of Cairngorm over the winter, and during the hours she had climbed on ice and rock with Sandy in Chamonix. The next day she and Patrick walked to the bottom of the Lhotse Face to take a closer look; it looked even more threatening close up.

It was quite overpowering. Very hard blue ice. *Very* steep, with few or no visible footholds. About two-thirds of the way up the face is Camp 3, perched on the edge of the steep face and open to the full force of the elements. The hill is getting serious now.

They planned to climb to Camp 3 the next day but the weather was beginning to turn against them. At six a.m. high winds were buffeting the tents, but they got up nevertheless.

Henry, Kevin, Ian and Rob set off first; Patrick and Vicky waited about an hour later, but just as they were leaving camp the others returned, forced back by the freezing temperatures and relentless wind. Vicky and Patrick decided they would still try their luck, but only got as far as within twenty minutes of the Face before they turned back. It was so cold that Vicky had smothered her head in a hood, hat, goggles and a neck scarf pulled up over her face. She could hardly breathe and wondered, resignedly, if that was how it would feel when the time came to wear her oxygen mask. When they got back to Camp 2, Henry had decided that the weather was too bad and they would return to Base Camp. It was as they were approaching Camp 1 that they heard the news: there had been an ice collapse in the Icefall while two Sherpas were crossing the big ladder at the top. One Sherpa had possibly broken his back and the other had injured his hip. The team waited at Camp 1 for further news; they knew they would be unable to get through until the men had been carried to safety and the ice doctors had repaired the ladder. But as time went by, the weather began to close in again and a decision was made to start moving. At the top of the Icefall, Henry said they should wait for further news, but Patrick wanted to push on and he and Vicky went on alone. They found three ice doctors still working on repairs, but they said it was OK to pass. Vicky was shaken by what she saw.

> It really was scary to see what had happened only a few hours earlier. Instead of two big horizontal ladders across a gap, it was now two vertical ladders and then a huge vertical ladder (made of five or six ladders lashed together) stretching up a massive block of ice. Patrick and I continued down. There was an eerie silence in the Icefall – nobody was coming up and there were dozens and dozens of abandoned Sherpa loads scattered all over. When a collapse happens, the Sherpas drop their loads and return to Base Camp, at least for the rest of that

day. It was as if the world had stopped and was waiting for something to happen.

Over the next few days everyone rested at Base Camp. There were varying weather reports coming in and Henry would not be drawn on when the next climb to Camp 3 would start. The plan was to go up to Camp 2 for about five days, and during that time climb to Camp 3, spend one night there and then return to Base Camp. That would complete the acclimatisation and everyone would by that time be ready for the summit. When that stage is reached, it's all about the weather, and the weather that year was very changeable. By 24 April the team was ready and packed for leaving the next morning, but in the evening Henry announced that the weather was still dicey and he was not confident about everyone going up the next day. There was some frank, and at times heated, discussion until eventually it was agreed that they would leave it for another day.

*　　*　　*　　*　　*

Saturday 26 April
Went up through the Icefall. The route had changed towards the top due to the collapse, but I wasn't too happy with the new route – it all seemed very unstable. At the start I wasn't going too well – it was the wrong time of the month and my tummy was cramping badly – Patrick was going too quickly for me, and eventually I collapsed on the ice in tears. Ian was great and helped me a lot, and Patrick took my rucksack for about five minutes, but it was silly so I insisted on taking it back. I struggled to the top of the Icefall and then the long trek across the plateau to Camp 2.

They were on their way at last to the Lhotse Face and Camp 3. A period was the last thing Vicky needed with this severe test looming ahead of her, but there was nothing to be done; it was just an extra burden to be carried up the hill. The rest days at Camp 2 helped, but she was apprehensive about the Lhotse Face and did not sleep well that night, or the next. But the dawn of Tuesday 29 April came and the team set off for the bottom of the Face. It glistened and glittered in the distance, rising massively from the tumble of snow and ice which marked the head of the Western Cwm glacier, the same glacier that collapsed into the Icefall below Camp 1. The Lhotse Face is, as its name suggests, one face of Everest's neighbouring mountain, Lhotse. If you were to continue up the Face, you would reach its summit; but if you are climbing Everest, you veer off the Face about three-quarters of the way up, cross the Yellow Band, climb over the Geneva Spur and then along into the South Col, which is the dip between Lhotse and Everest.

The bottom of the Face was terrifying – steep, hard and shiny and rearing up forever into the sky.

It was just so massive. None of us was comfortable. Ian was acutely ill at ease, as was Rob. I go very quiet when I'm under stress. I was terribly, terribly uncomfortable. It was like being in another world. This was just ice, ice, ice going up for miles. You could see up a few hundred feet at a time, and it took ages to move up. You had to stop and change from fixed rope to fixed rope, clipping on and off. I felt very insecure, and tried not to look down, and hoped my legs wouldn't start shaking with the effort of kicking into the ice for each step. But they did, and that's when you get what's called sewing machine leg – your leg wobbles up and down uncontrollably, just through sheer exertion and muscular strain. I was terrified that my crampon was going to jump out of the foothold. I was trying to keep my weight on my foot, but it was shaking and there was nothing I could do about it. And this was me hundreds and hundreds of feet up.

Vicky's energy levels were still very low, her blood sugar down, and every step was a punishing effort. She was breathing very hard, feeling as if her lungs were going to explode, pushing herself with every ounce of strength and willpower. At the top of every fixed rope, she had to rest and although Patrick was urging her on, she knew she was getting slower and slower. And then she began to hear a sound she has never forgotten: a high-pitched whistling as stones and small rocks dislodged by the climbers above shot down the mountain. The stones come careering down the face and if you're in the way, it's extremely dangerous. Two of the Sherpas who were climbing with them were hit badly on the shoulder and the arm, and every time Vicky heard the unearthly high-pitched whine above her she buried her head against the ice, her whole body tensed for the impact.

As the hours ground on, the wind began to rise, the clouds descended and it became very cold. Still they climbed, resting on the flatter bits, moving round outcrops, plodding up slopes, and they started to come across ruined tents flapping in the wind, the remains of previous camps which had been trashed by the storms. At last, they were getting near Camp 3, Vicky thought, but it still took another hour and a half. The slope went on and on. She began, for the first time, to think about dead bodies and wondered if she would see any. People had told her before she went to Everest that there are many bodies left on the mountain, frozen where they fell; here on the Lhotse Face, struggling for breath, she began to think of those people who had perished. Seven more climbers would die that year on the mountain.

Suddenly she saw a group of tents about 300 feet up. Those last few yards, through a mixture of ice and deep, soft snow, criss-crossed with crevasses, seemed to go on for ever but finally, finally, seven and a half hours after they left Camp 2, Vicky reached her tent which the Sherpas had carried up earlier, and collapsed inside. While she unpacked the kit and sorted out boots, mats and sleeping bags, Patrick set about collecting snow for melting. Kevin, who would also be sharing the tent, stumbled into camp about half an hour later. Tonight they would have to cook their own food as the Sherpas will not stay at Camp 3. It is a precarious site, perched high on the Lhotse Face, extremely vulnerable to avalanches and high winds. Patrick had boiled up snow and, concerned that Vicky had not drunk much during the climb, told her to drink her bottled water quickly. It was ice cold, but she drank what she could. He then gave her a mug of cup-a-soup. As soon as she had finished it, she lurched for the tent door and was sick. Although she felt very much better, Patrick was so concerned that he put her on oxygen at four litres per minute for half an hour. During the night she continued to feel cold and shivery, partly due to her period, partly from lack of food and fluid, exacerbated by the altitude, and Patrick gave her more oxygen for a couple of hours.

It was a freezing cold night, perched 24,500 feet up, on an exposed mountain face. Everyone felt awful and barely slept. At these altitudes, and with the punishing physical demands, you simply feel ill most of the time: you haven't got enough oxygen, you haven't got enough energy, your brain doesn't work properly and that frustrates you. You can't drink, you feel sick, you've got no saliva, you can't swallow food. So why on earth do it? Vicky always comes back to the sense of freedom and exhilaration the mountains give her, but how much freedom can there be in an environment where you can barely take a step without stopping to suck every last ounce of air from your aching lungs?

I know how difficult people find it to understand, but when you're up there, when you've recovered a bit and it's a day of blue, blue sky and sun and you can look out from high above the world, I have such a sense of privilege at being there. I've fought heck of a hard battle to get there, and the experience is immense, it's overpowering. It hits me hard, in the heart, and the pain just melts away. Why does anyone climb a hill? Why do I climb hills in bad weather? I can't explain it. I know I'm not going to get a view at the top, but I still want to get there. The pain of getting to Camp 3, or Camp 2 or through the Icefall – these were the things I had to do to get to the top, and I was going to the top of Everest. And it's not just about the destination; it's the journey as well. If I wasn't fixed on the destination, I wouldn't make the journey, but the travelling has wonderful, immense moments. I do think many important things in life happen in a split second. Climbing Everest is just the same: these moments of glorious vistas, or huge physical exhaustion; the powerful sense of release and freedom, and the sudden dangers and moments of fear. I think it probably sounds crass to say it, but when I'm up there I feel pure inside, as if I've been cleansed. I just feel that I'm in the right place. Yes, it's a dangerous environment and people lose their lives, and other people will feel differently. But for me, those feelings of freedom and goodness are very powerful and very uplifting.

Camp 3 had been reached, the acclimatisation climbs had been completed. The next morning they returned to Camp 2, overnighted and were back at Base Camp by the afternoon of Thursday 1 May. The next time they climbed the mountain, they would be aiming for the summit.

* * * * *

Most people climb Everest in the spring, usually reaching Base Camp at the end of March and trying for the summit sometime around the first couple of weeks of May, although the weather window can be later or earlier by as much as a week or more. It all depends on two or three days (usually in May and October) when the winds at the top of the mountain abate. Everest is so high that the upper slopes are battered by jet stream winds which would blow you off the mountain in a moment. Twice a year, though, the monsoon travelling from the Bay of Bengal carries warm, moist air northwards and when that air meets the Himalayas it is forced upwards. As it rises, it nudges the jet stream a few thousand feet higher and leaves the summit of Everest clear of the worst of the winds. When these few days will occur no one knows for sure; how long they will last is also a gamble. So everyone tries to be ready by the first week of May and Base Camp becomes a tense, expectant melee of climbers anxiously waiting for the latest weather forecasts.

The waiting can go on and on, so people often descend from Base Camp to the richer air of the foothills in order to build up strength. The drawback is that you may be wasting energy in walking down and back up again, or you may catch a germ, or you may miss the weather window if it comes suddenly. Vicky was unsure of what to do, but as everyone else in the team decided to go down, she joined them and walked down to Pangboche for a few days. The latest forecast suggested that very windy weather would continue for the next six days. They spent a relaxing few days wandering around Pangboche, then down to the rhododendron forests of Deboche and gradually wound their way back up to Base Camp, taking their time and arriving back at Base Camp in the late afternoon of 9 May. Vicky had been experiencing a few stomach problems and was rather tired but she thought no more about it until the next morning when she woke up and could not move.

I had no idea what was wrong. I simply could not move. I couldn't crawl out of the tent to get to the loo, I couldn't stand up. I began to think, 'If I can't move, I can't climb. I can't climb Everest.'

Her back had completely seized up, probably because of the long walk back up to Base Camp the day before when she had been hot and sweating; she had then sat in the mess tent, without a warm jacket, and her back muscles must have started to cool down and gone into spasm overnight. Whatever the reason, she was in no fit state to go anywhere. After a while she managed to crawl on her hands and knees to the loo, and then to the mess tent, and for the rest of the day people brought food to her tent. Rob was the camp doctor and he gave her some anti-inflammatory pills, but by the next day she was still in pain and barely able to walk.

Henry came to her tent later that day. He gave her a long look and took a deep breath.

'Vicky, I'm sorry but, if you're not any better by the time the weather forecast is OK for the summit, I'm afraid you won't be able to go.'

Vicky's heart sank, but she had already been going through all the scenarios in her mind, lying in her tent hour after hour.

'Well, what will be, will be,' was all she said. 'I know I can't climb if my back's not right.'

Henry was rather taken aback. He was used to long arguments and scenes with people who had invested so much time and money and passion in their quest to climb Everest, that any suggestion that someone was stopping them from achieving their dream was like a red rag to a bull; he was not used to this sort of stoicism. He thanked her for accepting that she might not get a chance to try for the summit. Vicky simply smiled. She didn't feel the least bit calm inside, but she was prepared to be patient; her back would improve enough for her to climb, or it wouldn't. And neither she nor Henry had the least control over that; she had no quarrel with Henry, and he was telling her nothing she did not already know.

Over the next couple of days her back did begin to ease, through a combination of rest, pills and an electrical pulse device called a TENS machine; Badia, a Mexican climbing friend, brought it to Vicky's tent and gave her several sessions on it. The weather was still not good for a summit bid, so it looked as if Vicky would be OK. But then Patrick received terrible news from home: his brother, who was a military pilot, had been killed in plane accident while on manoeuvres near Salt Lake City. He had to leave immediately to be with his family. It was a shocking end to the few weeks Vicky and Patrick and the team had spent together on the mountain; she was deeply upset for him and when he left a deep gloom and silence settled over the camp. Vicky would still try for the summit, but it would be without the guide who had helped, pushed and encouraged her; it was an unnerving prospect.

Days of frustration and boredom followed, as weather reports came in (at a cost of £200 each from the London Met Office), plans were made and changed, people got tenser and Henry was bombarded with questions about when the team was going to start for the summit. The team had packed and re-packed their kit several times in anticipation of leaving, but when the decision finally came, they went back to their tents and packed everything again: they would leave Base Camp on Saturday 17 May, with the intention of going for the summit on 20 or 21 May. Vicky's last diary entry reads:

Friday 16 May

Got packed for our summit bid tomorrow. Went to internet café and read some lovely emails from home; there were also lots expressing sympathy and kind thoughts for Patrick and his family. It was very moving and I found tears in my eyes again. I'm amazed how many people read my website and send emails. I posted another update and said I would be going for the summit soon and so everyone should expect silence for the next week to ten days.

* * * * *

They had reached Camp 3 and everyone put on their oxygen masks and slept with them on through the night. The masks were intensely uncomfortable to wear when resting, and even worse when climbing because the little plastic pipe running from the mask into the canister is rigid and every time you move your head, it pushes the mask up your face and causes your goggles to dig into your eyes. The more you dip your head to see where you are placing your feet, the more the oxygen mask pushes into the goggles. The mask is tight and constricting and the instinct is to rip it off immediately because you feel as if you can't breathe. Vicky had to use every ounce of will-power to stop herself clawing it off her face and, instead, to concentrate, concentrate, concentrate on putting one foot in front of the other. She climbed with her oxygen on a flow of three litres per minute – or as she called it, Gas Mark 3. But even at Gas Mark 3, any physical exertion at this altitude – 25,000 feet and higher – is crippling. The band above 26,000 feet is dramatically called the Death Zone; that is where the body is slowly dying because of lack of oxygen and all the attendant side effects: inability to eat and drink, exhaustion, slowing down of brain function, congealing of the blood and the risk of pulmonary or cerebral oedema, hypothermia from the intense cold. Humans were not designed to survive above the clouds.

The climb through the Icefall via Camp 2 and up the Lhotse Face to Camp 3 had been hard, but less severe than the time before. Vicky was hugely apprehensive that she would find the Lhotse Face as overpowering as it had been the first time, but it was slightly better: she was exhausted, of course, and it was gruelling, but at least she did not feel sick. As they set off from Camp 3 the next morning, bound for final camp in South Col, she was keyed up and anxious. She had slept very little the night before and today would be a truly gigantic climb: not only would they have to get to Camp 4, but once they arrived in the afternoon, they would rest for only a few hours before beginning the summit climb at nine o'clock that evening. In one day, with only three or four hours' rest, they would be climbing from 25,500 feet to 29,028 feet. Vicky kept chanting her personal mantra in her head: 'It's only a Munro. I can climb a Munro. I've got this far, I can climb another Munro.'

They left Camp 3, picking their way past the tents pitched precariously on the icy slopes, stepping over and round crevasses, and clipped on again to the fixed ropes continuing up the Ice Face. What happened next, happened very suddenly.

As we left it was quite steep, with boiler-plate ice. Rob was in front of me, kicking like billy-o, trying to get a grip on the ice. Suddenly he slipped and shot backwards, crashing straight into me and taking my legs from under me. We didn't fall far, just a messy slither, but it really unnerved me. I was uncomfortable enough, not being able to get a grip on the ice, and to be knocked down into the bargain was shocking. It wasn't a good start to the day.

They crossed diagonally over the Yellow Band and climbed towards the Geneva Spur, a big shoulder of rock which juts out from the mountain. At that point they were coming off ice and on to rock and Vicky was beginning to wilt, but ahead of them there was still the long, hard pull up over the Geneva Spur, before they would drop down into the South Col. The oxygen hissed in the pipe, and her own ragged breathing rasped and pounded in her head. Her goggles had frozen up and she could only see through a tiny little corner in the bottom right hand corner. She trudged on, her head bent to the side, trying to pick out the route, while ahead of her stretched a long line of people crawling up to the skyline.

By the time she reached the South Col she was almost staggering. It had taken six, seven, maybe eight hours from Camp 3. The Sherpas had previously set up the Camp and brought her hot lemon juice to drink, helped her take off her crampons and get into the tent. There is a photograph of her standing among the loose rocks and scree of the South Col, in her yellow down jacket, her mask off: her lips are blue from lack of oxygen. It is a bleak, desolate place, the South Col. Everest loomed above it, partially obscured by the clouds, and it was cold and windy. Here, for the next few hours, she would rest as best she could, trying to regain strength for the last 3,000-foot climb to the summit.

Because the weather, once again, was iffy, there was some discussion as to whether they would make the summit attempt. The wind was getting up, and Henry was getting regular updates from Base Camp by radio. He decided that they would go for it. It was the night of 21 May, Vicky's mother's birthday. Back at Base Camp, when they knew they would make an attempt around the 21st, Vicky had quietly delighted in the symmetry of it all: she would be going for the summit in the year of her fiftieth birthday, on the day of her mother's birthday, and fifty years after the first ascent of Everest. But it was not to be: they left at nine p.m. on 21 May, and would climb through the night so, if she reached the summit, it would be on 22 May. It had been a nice thought to carry with her, for a while.

They set off into the night. Because it was the fiftieth anniversary, and because the weather had been bad earlier in the month, Everest was especially busy. Vicky came out of the tent and saw a stream of headtorches, bobbing and flickering in the darkness, winding up the mountain to the Balcony. The Balcony is a slight ledge, halfway up to the summit, where fresh oxygen bottles had previously been stashed by the Sherpas. Vicky had two bottles in her pack. She would use about three quarters of a tank up to the Balcony, would replace that with a fresh one, and would have two full bottles to get her to the summit and back to the South Col. That was the plan, but in just a few hours time it would all go horribly wrong.

She set off with her Sherpa who would climb with her to the

summit, and come back down with her to the South Col. It was exhausting trudging up to the Balcony. Everyone was struggling in the darkness, panting for breath, following nose-to-tail up the ice, snow and rock. After a couple of hours Vicky saw Ian sitting at the side of the main trail, with his Sherpa standing over him. He looked done in. Vicky could not see where Rob and Kevin were, but she decided they must be ahead of her as they had set off first. The large numbers of people meant that the going was slow, which was good for catching your breath. It was still dark when she reached the Balcony, and sat down while her Sherpa rummaged about in her pack to change the oxygen bottle. 'I'm half-way there,' she kept repeating to herself. 'Half-way there.' She was vaguely aware that there was a lot of shouting in Nepalese going on behind her, between her Sherpa and some others, but she was too tired to care and when the bottle had been changed, she hauled herself to her feet and set off again up the ridge. Gradually she became aware of flashes of light behind her and she wondered who had the time or energy to take photographs. But it wasn't flash photography; it was lightning, far in the distance, illuminating the sky behind her in bursts of sudden brilliance. She plodded on and the darkness began to wash away as dawn crept across the sky. When she caught sight of the red blush on the horizon, she stopped and turned round. It was so beautiful that she cried.

As she and her Sherpa climbed higher and higher the wind began to pick up. Back at Base Camp they had been told that, if you're going up to the summit and the wind blows across you in either direction, don't worry too much about it; but if the wind is blowing straight down into your face, then it's time to be wary. Approaching the south summit, Vicky felt the wind begin to blow into her face, and around her the clouds started to close in. At this point, she was struggling. Her Sherpa kept urging her from behind to go faster and to overtake people, but she simply could not bring herself to unclip from the rope, not full, so both of them had set off for the summit with too little oxygen. Perhaps also, because of the weather and the numbers of people, it had all taken longer than it should have and they had used too much. The situation was clear now: 28,000 feet up and they had run out of oxygen. Although many details of the next few hours on the mountain are hazy in Vicky's memory, what happened just after the discovery about the oxygen remains engraved in her mind.

I'll never forget this. We both stood there, somewhere below the south summit, and my Sherpa pulled down his mask. He shouted to me through the wind: 'I die. You die. We both die. I go.' And off he went. He disappeared down the ridge. So there I was, left alone, no oxygen, in the high winds and cloud, with hardly any visibility. I can't say I felt angry about him; he had been very good with me up to that point, but he was just a young lad and you can't tell how people are going to react in adversity. I think he just lost his nerve. All I thought was: I've got to get down.

Vicky knew she had to get down, but very soon she began to suffer from the effects of lack of oxygen. She didn't feel particularly worried about anything and she believes now that it's because she was not fully conscious. She was virtually incapable of doing anything for herself, whether it was to take off her mask or to think about trying to find another bottle of oxygen when she eventually got to the Balcony. She didn't recognise where the Balcony was. She just blindly followed the ropes when she could find them, one thought in her mind: I have to get to the South Col.

At one point she remembers standing very near to an edge. She looked down over the precipice and thought, 'Oh, if I fall here I'll die,' but it barely registered. She had no angst, just a rather warm, cosy feeling. On she went. There were a couple of abseils over rocky outcrops which she remembered from the way up, and which she got down, but she cannot remember doing them or how in the world she managed to. Sometime later on she remembers she had sat down on a slightly less steep slope when she spotted two people emerging from the clouds. She was exhausted and desperate for something to drink since her last water had been the previous night, and she was too disoriented to think of taking off her pack and looking for her water bottle. When the two climbers came nearer she floundered over to them and asked for water, but either they couldn't understand her – she has a vague memory that they were Japanese – or had no water themselves and they did not give her any. This made her very angry, she remembers, and she became even more enraged when she saw them continuing up the mountain: why were they climbing to the summit when it was light? It was too late. They would die. Only later, when the clouds around her briefly parted, did she realise the full horror of her situation: she was so completely disoriented that it was *she,* and not the two Japanese, who was climbing up the slope. At some point she had turned around completely and was now struggling back up the mountain.

Vicky has no memory of how long she stumbled her way down to the South Col. Great chunks of those hours have disappeared from her mind. She even wonders whether the Japanese climbers were real, or whether, in her oxygen-deprived state, she imagined them. When she turned round again to go down, all she can remember are snatches: she was sitting, then trying to stand, walking a bit, falling over, sitting down again. Just sitting, doing nothing. She could barely walk because her muscles had seized up, and going downhill was agony.

Two Sherpas from Camp 4 were out looking for Vicky. Her own Sherpa must have arrived and told them what happened, and eventually, not far from the South Col, they found her. They helped her back, one on either side, but by this stage she was so far gone that, when they tried to take off her pack to carry it for her, she began shouting at them to leave her alone. They half-walked, half-carried her into Camp where she was put on oxygen right away and the next thing she knew it was morning.

When she awoke, they set off again. Vicky, who could barely put one foot in front of the other, had to drag herself out of her tent and make the long trek back to Camp 3. But she was, in her words, 'finished, shot to pieces' and by the time they reached Camp 3 she was incapable of going any further. Normally, coming down off the South Col, you would go straight through Camp 3 and on to Camp 2, but it was impossible for Vicky. Henry realised how serious the situation was and arranged for the two of them to stay in someone else's tent – the Sherpas had already gone on down – and they spent the night high up on the Lhotse Face.

It was while she was lying in the tent at Camp 3, that Vicky made her decision: she was going to come back the following year, and this time she would get to the top. Perversely, there was a part of her that was almost glad she hadn't made it the first time, because it gave her an excuse to come back to this terrifying, beautiful place which had got inside her so deeply that she desperately wanted, needed, to return. She would be able to enjoy the camaraderie of Base Camp again, to see all the Sherpas and porters again, to watch the moon pouring its light on to the Icefall again. To try again to realise her dream.

*   *   *   *   *

Vicky saw her Sherpa again, once, in Kathmandu. There were huge celebrations in the city to mark the fiftieth anniversary of the 1953 ascent and, although she was delighted to be there, she was still far too tired to take part. She was happy to rest in her hotel room, luxuriating in a double bed and being able to take a hot shower whenever she wanted. When she had finally got back to Base Camp, the rest of the team had already left, the tents had been dismantled and her gear all packed away, so Henry arranged for her to stay in a spare tent belonging to another expedition. She couldn't face the twenty-six-mile walk back to Lukla, so when she heard that there was a helicopter already arranged to take other people off the mountain, she paid for a seat and was flown back to Lukla in comfort.

One afternoon, when the festivities were at their height, there was a knock on her hotel room door. She thought it was Kevin or Ian, but there was her Sherpa, with one of the other Sherpas from the trip. He had come to ask for his tip. It was normal for climbers to tip the Sherpas, but Vicky was rather taken aback. Still, she had no ill-feeling towards him, so, in the spirit of the festivities of the day, she gave him something. The look on his face told her it wasn't enough but, well, she wasn't feeling *that* generous.

She was not in the least depressed about missing the summit. It was simply that she had no energy. The hours she wandered about on the mountain had severely drained her and she believes, to this day, that her memory has been permanently affected by being oxygen-depleted for so long. But she was elated at the prospect of coming back and trying again.

I had a deep inner belief that I could do it. I didn't feel about Everest, 'It's beaten me, I'm not going back.' Maybe it was because I don't remember big chunks of it and, over time, Nature protects you by blotting things out. All that mattered was that I had had a great time, despite everything. It was fine. I was coming back.

11

ON TOP OF THE WORLD

The letter is written on lined paper in a neat biro hand. It is dated 5 June 2003 and the address in the top left hand corner is Park School, Oban. Vicky received it on her return from Everest and has kept it ever since, in its now rather battered brown envelope.

Dear Vicky Jack,

We are writing to say we are very, very pleased to hear that you are back home safe and well. You must have been really excited on your journey to Everest. What was it like? Were you frightened? I'm sure Keri and I would be scared. We know for certain that you shall never forget your visit to Everest as long as you live.

When you were climbing Everest we were following your progress in the Herald. All of our school is very proud of your wonderful achievement and you must be too! Do you have any plans to go to Nepal to try for the summit again?

When you were climbing Everest we were climbing waterfalls at Castle Toward. We were at Castle Toward for four days, it was great fun. Just in case you don't know, Castle Toward is an outdoor centre near Dunoon. We all really liked the activities. You never know, one of us might be as good a mountaineer as you are one day!

Best wishes for the future,
Katy, Keri, Mrs Ross and P7

It was a beautiful letter to receive. Vicky had no idea when she set off for Everest that twenty-four schoolchildren in Oban had been following her story. Enclosed with the letter was a photograph of the entire class in front of an enormous poster, headed 'Well done, Vicky' in huge blue capitals, and surrounded by photos of Everest and Vicky and cuttings from the newspapers. Three pupils kneeling in the front row were also holding their own pencil and ink drawings, two of mountains and one of Vicky on a summit, which they sent with the letter.

The letter was special because it was so unexpected, and the youngsters had obviously put a great deal of time and effort into their Vicky Jack project, but it was only one of dozens of letters and cards she received when she got home. Everyone was so delighted and relieved that she was back safely: neighbours, climbing friends, work colleagues. The achievement had been in attempting the climb and coming down again safely; the fact that she had not reached the summit seemed hardly to matter, especially since Vicky said she was, of course, going to try again. No one was in the least surprised.

She was still pretty tired and spent when she got home, though, and the first thing she did was to go on holiday to Canada where she spent a few weeks with Alan Dennis, the climber who had taken her into the Cairngorms the previous winter to climb and assist on avalanche work. On her return she threw herself into the project she had been planning during idle hours in her tent at Everest Base Camp: the re-building and re-decorating of the cottage at Balquhidder. This was to take up virtually all her time until she returned to Everest in March 2004. For the next nine months she and friends, including Alan, who came over from Canada, Ron Swanson from Forres, and her neighbour Roni Hamilton from along the road, set to work on knocking down walls, pulling up floorboards, laying new concrete floors and re-flooring them, stripping walls of lath and plaster and transforming the cottage. When the builders came on the scene, Vicky became Clerk of Works and, never one to do anything half-heartedly, managed the project from dawn till dusk. At one point she had she neither wanted nor needed a guide, and she felt much more confident that she could get to the South Col by herself. But that did not mean that she had any less respect for the mountain, or that entering the Icefall each time did not cause her to draw breath deeply and concentrate all her energies and skill on making sure that she did not put a foot wrong. And there were incidents and accidents. One of her climbing companions was John Wylie, a mechanical engineer from Tasmania who was studying for a philosophy degree in his spare time. He and Vicky often climbed with Bob Jen, a real-estate business entrepreneur from New York who was a very accomplished climber, tennis player and marathon runner. On one trip through the Icefall, Vicky and John came to a truly gigantic crevasse which was crossed by five horizontal ladders lashed together. Vicky wobbled across and waited on the other side for John. To her horror she saw him take two or three steps, lose his balance and fall off the ladder. Somehow his ice axe became wedged between two of the rungs, trapping his foot, so John was hanging below the ladder, upside down, completely helpless. He could neither pull himself up on his fixed rope, nor reach up to free his foot. Vicky knew that if she tried to re-cross the ladder and pull out the ice axe, the ladder would shake and sway and she would fall off as well. So she shouted to two Sherpas, who were just ahead, and they came running. Quick as a flash they danced across the ladder, light as acrobats, and released John's leg, so that he could haul himself up the fixed rope to safety. His ice axe dropped like a stone, hundreds of feet into the icy pit. Vicky shuddered with the fresh realisation that in this hostile environment, the slightest trip, the tiniest moment's loss of concentration, a sudden visitation of bad luck, and disaster could pounce.

So although Everest was familiar to her, it was no less dangerous or nerve-racking. The people in the team were different, and certainly her own focus and sense that she had some valuable experience under her belt were perhaps even stronger this year, but the mountain itself remained the same: glorious, overpowering, magnificent and deadly. One night at Camp 1 there was an avalanche which narrowly missed the tents which were pitched in the shadow of the left-hand mountain side of the Western Cwm. Vicky was sharing with Sue, Henry Todd's wife, when there was a sudden explosion of sound from nearby.

> Sue and I grabbed each other – we didn't know what was happening. The sound was like a deep rumble, getting louder and louder. There was some shouting around us from outside, and a voice – Henry's, I think – yelling at us to stay in the tent. Suddenly the tent was flattened on top of us, and there were screams, and then the tent stood up again, and a few seconds later was flattened again. Sue knew what was happening, but I didn't: an avalanche displaces a huge rush of wind in front of it, and when it stops, there's a huge rush of wind back. Because we were so near, the gust of wind flattened our tent twice, and we were showered with snow.

When they peeked out of the tent, they could see where the avalanche had dumped hundreds of tons of snow some distance away. Sue and Vicky got on well together and although Sue had a great deal more technical climbing experience, both women shared an intense determination and passion to get to the top of the mountain. Sue is slightly built, like Vicky, and she wrote recently on the website for Henry's ICE 8000 company about how physical strength is ultimately less important than mental drive when it comes to climbing Everest:

> I would suggest that only those people that have great mental strength generally succeed. Those that have the will and mental strength to push themselves where not many have gone before

them; not many out of the millions of people on this Earth have stood on the summit of Mount Everest. None of us knows what climbing to 8,848 metres will do to our bodies and our minds. Can we push our bodies that far, that high, will we get frostbite, will we succumb to lack of oxygen, or physical exhaustion? Will we die? All these doubts have to be mentally overcome on the way to the summit. If we cannot deal with them, then our minds will find an excuse for turning back. Obviously some people do have genuine life-threatening physical difficulties, and have to turn around. But there are others who decide the risks are not worth taking, that there are other things in their lives more important than climbing Everest – and no one can blame them for this. In order to climb Mount Everest you have to REALLY want it. It is not a mountain to be underestimated . . . and I believe some people do – because it has become more commercialised, because you can pay to climb it, without having climbed all your life, because people like that do climb it, because a slightly built girl like me can climb it – but that doesn't make it easy, that doesn't mean it isn't the hardest thing you will ever do in your life.

Vicky knew this long before she set foot on Everest. She knew that the years she spent climbing three or four Munros in one day, in all weathers from sunshine to snowstorms, were building up not just her muscles, but her inner steel and her mental toughness. She knew how much of climbing to the top is in the head, not just in the legs. And other people could sense her quiet determination and unquenchable will. Bob Jen remembers that his first impression of Vicky was of a relaxed, self-effacing person, but the more he saw of her, particularly when climbing, the more clearly he saw 'the meticulousness, the calculation of how to achieve her goal, the determination, the strong-mindedness'. 'She's a planner,' he says, 'and mentally very, very tough.' They often climbed together and grew to like each other, and they still keep in touch. There is a bond between those who have endured the hardships and enjoyed the fellowship of climbing Everest, which is not easily broken. Simon Piper, a GP from England, was also in the team. He first met Vicky in Kathmandu and found her 'fairly quiet', but good company. Like Bob Jen, he realised, when he began to climb with Vicky, that her mild manner hid something much tougher. 'Beneath the surface is a very strong, steely will,' says Simon. 'And she was also very strong physically, very fit.'

Simon could also see in Vicky the same passionate delight at being in the high mountains as he himself has always felt. He started climbing in his spare time in the late 1980s, after his family grew up, but he always loved mountains and skiing and worked in Switzerland for a couple of seasons as a young man. A few years ago he climbed Mont Blanc with his son, and then got his first taste of the Himalayas on the glorious Ama Dablam. Next he intends to climb Cho Oyu. Simon is eloquent about why he spends so much time and effort on climbing in the high places of the world. Not only are these mountains beautiful and magnificent, but being on them is 'a total escape' from the pressures of his job as a GP. Most of all, he says, climbing mountains 'is a reduction of life to simple things: you either go up, or down, or stay where you are. You eat, sleep and you go to the loo. It is a clear window of simplicity in one's life. In a way it must appeal to a primitive part of one's soul.'

For Vicky and the team on Everest, the pattern of climbing was the same as the previous year: repeated forays up and down the mountain, further each time and coming down again to Base Camp to recover. Weather conditions varied enormously from day to day and the Icefall, particularly, was extremely unstable. Vicky's email postings on her website describe how each time she goes through the Icefall, there has been yet another collapse, gigantic blocks of ice have shifted or tumbled and more massive gashes have opened in the snow. When the team set off on their climb to Camp 3 at the beginning of May, they were pinned down at Camp 2 for four days by storms. On the fifth day the wind abated a little so they decided to try their luck on the Lhotse Face, but high winds forced them back down to Camp 2 after they had climbed about 500 feet. When they eventually got back to Base Camp after reaching Camp 3, Henry decided that they should go down to a lower altitude, regain some strength and then return in five days or so to wait for a weather window to make their bid for the summit.

The wait at Base Camp was, as it had been the previous year, a mixture of tension, boredom and sociability. Everyone coped differently with the frustrations of waiting around for the weather to be right. Vicky spent a lot of time checking over her kit, reading, listening to music, updating her website, wandering over to other tents to meet other climbers and chat over food, and spending time with Bob Jen and John Wylie. Ted Atkins was another member of the big Henry Todd expedition, a serving RAF Aerosystems (aircraft) Engineering Officer, and in the days before the summit attempt he was busily continuing work on a new oxygen system which he was developing for high-altitude climbing. Others spent their time playing cards and board games, or sitting outside in the sun, or going for walks. It was all about patience and biding your time.

*   *   *   *   *

The moment had come. On 12 May, at three o'clock in the morning, Vicky pulled on her boots, zipped up her tent for the last time and emerged into the darkness. Under a vast glittering sky, Base Camp was alive with the noise of boots crumping over rocks, stones and ice, Sherpas calling, the occasional laugh and shouted remark from teams of climbers already plodding towards the Icefall. As she joined the others, tense with excitement and aching to get going, Vicky told herself, 'You can do this, because you did it last year. You nearly got to the top. You will get there this time.'

Through the Icefall, eerie and beautiful in the moonlight, up past Camp 1, and then the long slog up the Western Cwm to Camp 2, Bob in front, then John and then Vicky. They stayed two nights at Camp 2, recovering and gaining strength for the long haul up the Lhotse Face to Camp 3. Compared with the previous year, Vicky found the climb significantly less debilitating. It still pushed her to her limits, but she coped much better. But it was a tough night in the tent. Vicky was sharing with Sue Todd and they had a pretty miserable time of it, perched high on the mountain side. The platforms for the tents are hacked out of the ice so they are very uneven, and when the warmth of people's bodies begins to melt the ice, little ridges form which are extremely uncomfortable to lie on. Sue remembers that when they arrived:

> The tent was full of oxygen cylinders, and partly buried in the snow. We were exhausted when we got there, and then we had to melt snow for drinks etc. We didn't really have room to stretch out and I don't think either of us got much sleep. It was a total nightmare in fact!

The next morning they set off for the South Col. Vicky thinks she started off with Sue, Bob and John but, at that altitude, cocooned in her oxygen mask, gasping for every breath and focusing just on putting one foot in front of another, she was basically in a world of her own. She could see the route, and the line of people ahead of her, and she just kept going. At the South Col, she felt much stronger than the year before:

> It was a different league altogether. A big, big difference. I won't say I skipped into the South Col – it was hard, hard work – but I wasn't labouring and slowing to a dead-stop like

I was the year before. It was almost as if my body had remembered being at altitude the year before and had adapted. And when I got into the tent with Sue, we experienced a surge of excitement: 'We're going for the top!'

After a few hours' rest in the tent, they set off again at nine o'clock at night, up the long, long climb to the Balcony.

Sue set off before me, with her Sherpa and I followed with mine. I remember crossing the rocky ground of the South Col to the first band of ice. And then there's this long haul up to the Balcony, on snow and ice all the way, that gets steeper. All this kit on, it's night-time, and my head torch is only showing a tiny patch of ground in front of me. I'm grinding out the steps behind a long line of people.

I got really tired as this went on and at one stage I thought: 'What on earth am I doing here? Do I really want to get to the top of this hill? Maybe I'm not that bothered.' That was the first time on any of the Seven Summits that I've felt like that. It just flashed through my mind. And then I regained concentration and said to myself: 'Pull yourself together, Vicky, and get on with it. Don't be so stupid. Put that out of your mind.' And on I went.

She reached the Balcony and her Sherpa changed her oxygen cylinder. They set off up the ridge which the year before had so scared her that she could not bring herself to unclip and clip back on to the rope so that she could pass people who were ahead of her. This time she felt much more comfortable – until the dawn came, just when she reached the south summit and, for the first time, she saw the summit ridge rearing up into the sky ahead of her.

I could see mountains and peaks all around me. The vista was enormous and breathtaking. And then I looked up at the summit ridge and thought, with a sharp intake of breath, 'That looks awful. I'll never be able to do that.' I turned to my Sherpa and said, 'I don't know that I can manage the summit ridge.' He looked at me and smiled and said, 'You will be fine. You stay with me. I help you.'

The thing was, Vicky had never seen the summit ridge before. The previous year there had been virtually no visibility, with the storm rising and the clouds smothering the summit. Now, for the first time, she could see the ridge climbing to the sky, steep and corniced with snow, the mountain sloping down for thousands of feet on one side, and disappearing into airy nothingness on the other. To a woman who does not like heights, it looked very, very scary.

Her Sherpa was marvellous and helped her whenever she needed it. They made steady progress, down off the south summit, up over the Hillary Step and finally, finally, they were on the snowy slope up to the summit. Those last 600 feet seemed to take forever. Vicky remembers seeing Sue pass on her way down from the summit, looking easy and strong. Just a few more feet now. She could see the top, and the prayer flags fluttering in the wind, and the blue of the sky. Her heart was pounding, the breath ragged and rasping, and inside the excitement was mounting. For the first time she allowed the thought to flower sweetly in her head: 'I'm going to make it.'

Everything would have been fine if it had not been for a group of climbers who were already sitting on the summit. In her exhausted state, struggling for breath and barely able to think clearly, Vicky saw the climbers as a last obstacle which she was incapable of getting past. The summit of Everest is small, just a six foot-square table-sized mound like a rounded cone, which slopes steeply all around. In the middle there were two pictures of the Dalai Lama, a framed one placed on the ground and another smaller one on the end of a little metal pole sticking up from the snow. Prayer flags fluttered a foot or so above the ground. Vicky realised she would have to get round the climbers already there, but the sides were steep and she suddenly stopped: she couldn't do it. Her Sherpa realised what was happening, and he gently but firmly led her, unroped, round the edge of the climbers to the other side. As she picked her way gingerly, all Vicky could think was: 'If I trip now, that's it.' Everything was magnified in her mind and out of proportion. She was working so hard, her heart and lungs pumping so hard, and her brain working so slowly.

Once she was round, she sat down immediately. She felt as if she would fall otherwise. Only after a few minutes did she realise that she had inadvertently sat on the Dalai Lama, when she saw the corner of his photograph peeking out from underneath her. She had made it. She was on the summit of Everest, sitting on top of the highest place on the planet, but at first it was all too overwhelming.

I couldn't look at the view, because it was all too scary. I was perched on top of the highest mountain in the world and I wasn't feeling secure. I was sitting, hunched up, puffing and panting and with no idea of what to do next. My Sherpa helped me to take off my goggles, pulled my hood back, got my camera out of my pack and said, 'Smile, Vicky. Look at me!' I could hardly bring myself to lift my eyes and look at the camera. I was so high, so exhausted, and almost overcome by the enormity of where I was.

And then it all changed. I remember saying to myself, 'Come on, you are on the top of Mount Everest and you will never be back here again. Look up.' That moment of sanity hit and I looked up and out.

The whole of Tibet was spread beneath her, looking northwards. It was tremendous and unforgettable. She was sitting on top of Everest. All around, as far as the eye could see, were range upon range of snowy peaks, and huge glaciers in the distant valleys. Above her, the endless firmament. Inside her, a world too great and too intensely experienced to be easily explained in words.

It's just so hard to describe what happened when I looked up. I felt a warm glow rise inside me, and I was swamped by a glorious feeling of inner calm. Things settled in me that have remained settled. I can't explain where the settled feeling came from. It wasn't, 'I've done it. I'm here.' Or, 'I've finished the Seven Summits.' It was much, much deeper than that. It wasn't as if I'd met with Mum and Dad, but it was nearer to that than a feeling that I'd done the Seven Summits. But it wasn't that either. I felt close to them, but it was more than that. It was indescribable. I'd experienced something which will never leave me and which I will always treasure.

Vicky Jack reached the summit of Mount Everest at 08.15 on 16 May 2004. She became the first Scotswoman to complete the Seven Summits and the oldest British woman to reach the top of Everest. The journey to which she had devoted almost seven years of her life was complete.

EPILOGUE

Ithaca gave you the splendid journey.
Without her you would not have set out.

From 'Ithaca', by C. P. Cavafy (1911)
From *Collected Poems* (1990), translated
by Edmund Keeley and Philip Sherrard

When Vicky drove up the winding, single track road to the cottage on 3 June, the sight which greeted her brought tears to her eyes: a group of neighbours and friends from the glen, about fourteen of them, stood at the top of her driveway, under a big banner with 'WELCOME HOME, VICKY' emblazoned across it. First to rush up and envelop her in a huge hug were Tommy and Betty Macgregor. Tommy had organised the welcome reception. He had erected the poles on either side of the driveway to hold up the banner, found a big old rectangle of carpet and written on the back of it, and organised all the neighbours to be there at precisely two o'clock for Vicky's return. He and Betty had set up a long table loaded with bottles and glasses, and everyone cheered and clapped when Vicky's car appeared round the corner. The first bottle to be opened was champagne brought by Roni and Maureen Hamilton, Vicky's great friends from along the road who had looked after her so well before both Everest trips, with plenty of home-cooking and warm hospitality. Their wee grandson, Ruaridh, staggered up to Vicky with a huge bouquet of flowers which was bigger than himself, and the local news sheet, *The Villagers,* captured the moment on camera.

Tommy and Betty had been planning this ever since their phone rang on 19 May and, to their delight and disbelief, Vicky's voice floated down the line: 'It's me, Vicky! I'm at Base Camp. I've done it! I got to the top of Everest!' Vicky's voice was pulsating with energy and well-being. She emailed several people when she got back to Base Camp, but her first thought was a phone call to Tommy and Betty, her nearest neighbours, her mother's close friends. Now that she was finally back home, she could luxuriate in being in her own place again, safe and in one piece, with the excitement and achievement of climbing Everest still glowing deep within her. Many other members of the team had also reached the summit, including Sue Todd, John Wylie and Bob Jen. Vicky and Bob had not seen each other at the summit, nor even at the South Col. As Bob says, at that altitude, with all energies focused on the final push, 'I was in my own world, and she was in hers.' Bob still thinks of the summit day. He will never forget seeing the curvature of the earth from the highest point on the planet. And he'll always remember the evening, once they were all back in Kathmandu, when he went with Vicky to a famous restaurant called Rumdoodle, where they signed their names on the wall which is covered with the signatures of Everest summiteers: now their names appear alongside Sir Edmund Hillary, Reinhold Messner, Chris Bonington and a host of others.

As she wandered around her garden, delighting in the flowers which had been bulbs hidden beneath the ground when she had left for Everest, and breathing in the green perfume of the leaves which had been tight, hard buds back in March, Vicky felt enormously alive and strong. After being so long at high altitude, she was still energised by the masses of extra red blood cells which her body produced on Everest to try and absorb every last drop of oxygen; back at a low altitude, her body was saturated with oxygen and she felt fantastically powerful and heady with energy. And there was also pleasure in the delight and congratulations of friends, and in the dozens of letters and emails which arrived every day from all kinds of people, including a man who had been a boyhood friend of her brother Brian and whom she had not seen since she was ten.

The newspapers were full of her success and she featured in the headlines for many days after the summit news came through: 'I don't have a head for heights – but I climbed Everest!'; 'The ascent of a woman'; 'Vicky's on top of the world'. As many climbers have found, Everest was the mountain which attracted media attention, not the other Seven Summits: it was only when Everest loomed that the newspapers began to take an interest. And it was Everest which brought her notoriety in the professional sphere, too. More companies were interested in her, she received more offers of work, and business contacts would phone up and ask if she would like to come and talk about her experiences. Vicky is in no doubt that climbing Everest has raised her profile and helped her in developing her own business.

As for the significance of what she has achieved over the past seven years, and whether it has changed her in any profound way, Vicky is, not surprisingly for someone who does not like to dwell on the past or talk very much about her feelings, careful and understated. She will admit that she has changed over the years, but is not sure how much it has to do with climbing the Seven Summits.

> I feel much more comfortable within myself. I still give myself quite a hard time, though. I'm looking for the flaws. I don't like to pat myself on the back, because I always feel that's courting disaster. Looking back, I think that attitude sometimes swamped me, whereas now, it doesn't. Maybe that's just maturity and life.

The great joy has been the journey, the journey with a purpose and a destination. That has been the real meaning of these seven years of Vicky's life:

They've been marvellous, unbelievable. It's the journeys, the adventures and the experiences, and the going to places I would never have dreamt of: Antarctica, Alaska, the Indonesian jungle. And the friendships and the laughs, the highs and the lows – they mean so much. And the real satisfaction of coming down off a hill, having been to the top. It's terribly important to me to have things to look forward to, and I do need a goal and a challenge. Otherwise I can feel as if I'm standing still, and I hate that. But having said that, do I dwell on my experiences and think about them? Yes, I do, but they're separate cameos of experience. There's a whole tapestry of different feelings and experiences, each too precious to sweep up into a summary of the Seven Summits. I won't pull it together and say, 'That's the feeling, that's the meaning.' But it's just glorious, and I wouldn't have swapped it for anything.

In her thirties Vicky had a dream to climb all the Munros. She achieved that, and then her dream was: I'm going to climb the highest hill in Europe. On the way down from the summit of Mount Elbrus, the third dream emerged – to climb the Seven Summits, and, at the end of it, get to the top of Mount Everest. Each time she achieved a dream, the little voice at the back of her mind began to whisper: What next? Vicky admits, with a laugh, that it was not long at all after her return from Everest that she began to ask herself the question. A lot of other people were asking it, too, because at the end of her talks on the Seven Summits, someone always poses the question: 'What are you going to do next? What are your plans?'

As this goes to press, Vicky's immediate plan is to climb Mount Cook, the highest mountain in New Zealand. She is looking forward to it very much. And, on the way to New Zealand, she is going to stop off in Australia and climb the 'eighth' of the Seven Summits: Kosciuszko, the 7,310-foot hill in New South Wales. This is the mountain on the Dick Bass list, the alternative to Carstensz Pyramid. Vicky has completed her Seven Summits but, if there's another one to climb, she'll climb it . . .

But that is not a dream. At the moment, the dream is not formed, and Vicky does very much need another dream, another quest. She says she loves the Scottish hills and will continue to go up them for as long as she is able. She will climb the bigger mountains as long as the focus is there and she really has the drive and appetite and fitness for it. But, as for the big dream: who knows? Something else will beckon. Her gaze will fix on some other point on the horizon, and she will travel towards it, positively and happily.

I'll come up with something. I don't know what it is. I don't even know if it's about hills. But it will be something that gives me a place to go towards, a destination. I don't like to do things by halves, so whatever it is I want to throw myself into it. I won't commit until I've really found what I need and want to do. And then I'll do it from the heart.